Presented to:

By:

Date:

MY PERSONAL PROMISE BIBLE FOR TEENS

Honor Books
Tulsa, Oklahoma

My Personal Promise Bible for Teens
ISBN 1-56292-387-0
45-253-00261

P.O. Box 55388
Tulsa, Oklahoma 74155

Manuscript preparation and personalization of scriptures by Betsy Williams, Tulsa, Oklahoma.

MAKING GOD'S WORD PERSONAL

I had what some might call a "crisis of faith," although that sounds a bit grand for a thirteen-year-old's first doubts.

Still, age has nothing to do with a crisis, and the subject was my faith. Perhaps it resulted from unanswered prayer. I had begged God (and my parents) to let me go home. Without success. Or it may have been spiritual growing pains. Like the young man who went to a delightfully sane bishop to confess he had lost his faith. "Nonsense," replied the bishop. "You've lost your parents' faith. Now go out and get one of your own." I knew God had sent His Son, Jesus, to die for the sins of mankind, but somehow I did not feel included. There were so many and I was only one and, let's face it, not a very significant one at that. I prayed for forgiveness and felt nothing. I wasn't even sure He was listening.

Finally, in desperation, I went to my ever-practical sister, Rosa, and asked her advice. "I don't know what to tell you to do," she replied matter-of-factly, "unless you take some verse and put your own name in. See if that helps." So I picked up my Bible and turned to Isaiah 53, one of my favorite chapters. I did just what she suggested—I read, "He was wounded for [Ruth's] transgressions, He was bruised for [Ruth's] iniquities: the chastisement of [Ruth's] peace was upon Him; and with His stripes [Ruth] is healed" (see Isaiah 53:5).

I knew then that I was included.[1]

—Ruth Bell Graham

---

[1] Ruth Bell Graham, *It's My Turn,* published by Fleming H. Revell, a division of Baker Book House Company, copyright 1982.

INTRODUCTION

What if all the great and glorious promises of God had your name written right on them? Well, they do! God meant every God-breathed word to be His personal message to *you.*

Here are some practical tools for your spiritual journey—precious promises that teens need most, arranged under convenient topics. Each verse comes from the King James Bible, and whenever possible, we have carefully personalized the language either by using "I," "my," and "me" or by putting it into God's voice speaking to you. For example, "God has not given us a spirit of fear" has become "God, You have not given me the spirit of fear" or "I have not given you the spirit of fear." Experience the impact of God's love for you, the same way Ruth Bell Graham did as a young girl.

The additional affirmations, meditations, and Bible reading, as well as stories of great young people in the Bible and their prayers will also uplift you as a teen.

We pray that as you bring the Scripture into your daily life, God will empower you to become the young man or woman you desire to be with a renewed sense of God's loving, *personal* commitment to you, His child. God bless you as you discover the protection and the power of God's promises to *you!*

TABLE OF CONTENTS

My Personal Promise Bible for Teens

How to Use My Personal Promise Bible

Jesus said, "The words that I speak to you are spirit, and they are life" (John 6:63 NKJV). One of the most effective ways to experience a miraculous change in your life—the kind of change that will make you even better than you are now—is to allow God's words to sink deep into your heart through meditation, personalization of Scripture, and prayer. How?

Take a verse and memorize it. God's truth in you can then open your eyes to His great love for you. To get that truth to an even deeper, life-changing level, take that verse and think on it all day. Ask yourself, "How does this truth affect my life today?"

Next, make these promises personal. Any passage of Scripture can be personalized by inserting the personal pronouns *I, me,* and *my* into it, just as Ruth Bell Graham did. When you do this, God's truth becomes His truth *to you,* and you begin to experience lasting change in your life.

The final step is to pray these promises back to God. God's promises are His personal assurances to you. Not only will you be transformed by Him; you will become a spiritual encouragement in the lives of many others.

A Christ-like Heart Reflects God's . . .

*W*ithout God,
the world
would be a
maze without a clue.
Woodrow Wilson

This God is our God forever and ever;
He will be our guide even to the end.

Psalm 48:14 NIV

A Christ-like Heart Reflects God's . . .

Caring

You are my hiding place; You will preserve me from trouble; You will surround me with songs of deliverance.

Psalm 32:7

I will trust in You at all times; I pour out my heart before You. You, God, are a refuge for me.

Psalm 62:8

I am happy who have You, the God of Jacob, for my help. My hope is in You, LORD my God. . . . You execute judgment for me when I am oppressed. You give food to me when I am hungry. You loose me when I am a prisoner. You open my eyes when I am blind. You raise me when I am bowed down. You, LORD, love the righteous. You, preserve me when I am a stranger. You relieve the fatherless and widow, but the way of the wicked You turn upside down.

Psalm 146:5,7-9

CARING

They shall be ashamed and also humiliated, all of them; they shall become confused that are makers of idols. But Israel shall be saved in You, LORD, with an everlasting salvation. I shall not be ashamed nor humiliated, world without end.

Isaiah 45:16-17

Though I walk in the midst of trouble, You will revive me. You shall stretch forth Your hand against the wrath of my enemies, and Your right hand will save me.

Psalm 138:7

In the time of trouble, You will hide me in Your pavilion; in the secret of Your tabernacle You will hide me; You will set me up upon a rock.

Psalm 27:5

No one is useless in this world who lightens
the burden of it to anyone else.

Charles Dickens

A Christ-like Heart Reflects God's . . .

Commitment

I am blessed because I keep Your testimonies and seek You with my whole heart.

Psalm 119:2

"My eyes shall be upon the faithful of the land, that they may dwell with Me; the one who walks in a perfect way, this one shall serve Me."

Psalm 101:6

Your statutes, LORD, are right, rejoicing my heart. Your commandment is pure, enlightening my eyes. . . . Moreover by them I, Your servant, am warned, and in keeping them there is great reward.

Psalm 19:8,11

"Commit your way to Me, the LORD; trust also in Me, and I shall bring it to pass."

Psalm 37:5

"If you will be willing and obedient, you shall eat the good of the land."

Isaiah 1:19

"Wait on Me, your LORD, and keep My way, and I shall exalt you to inherit the land."

Psalm 37:34

COMMITMENT

You honor me who fears You, LORD. I swear to my own hurt and change not . . . if I do these things I shall never be moved.

Psalm 15:4-5

I love You, LORD, for You preserve the faithful, and plentifully reward the proud doer.

Psalm 31:23

All Your paths, LORD, are mercy and truth to me as I keep Your covenant and Your testimonies.

Psalm 25:10

You shall keep me, O LORD; You shall preserve me from this generation forever.

Psalm 12:7

"I am with you always, even to the end of the world."

Matthew 28:20

I make it a rule of Christian duty never to go to a place where there is not room for my Master as well as myself..

John Newton

A Christ-like Heart Reflects God's . . .

Compassion

You will turn again, You will have compassion on me; You will subdue my offenses, and You will cast all my sins into the depths of the sea.

Micah 7:19

You have made Your wonderful works to be remembered. You, LORD, are gracious and full of compassion.

Psalm 111:4

Because my heart was tender and I have humbled myself before You, LORD, . . . You also have heard me.

2 Kings 22:19

This I recall to my mind, therefore I have hope. It is of Your mercies, LORD, that I am not consumed, because Your compassions fail not. They are new every morning; great is Your faithfulness.

Lamentations 3:21-22

"Can a woman forget her sucking child, that she should not have compassion on the son of her womb? Behold I have engraved you on the palms of My hands; your walls are continually before Me."

Isaiah 49:15-16

Compassion

To me, the upright, there arises light in the darkness. You are gracious, and full of compassion, and righteous.

Psalm 112:4

It shall come to pass, after You have plucked us out, You will return and have compassion on me and will bring me again with every one to my heritage and with every one to my land.

Jeremiah 12:15

You, Lord, are very compassionate and of tender mercy.

James 5:11

You, O Lord, are a God full of compassion, and gracious, longsuffering, and plenteous in mercy and truth.

Psalm 86:15

I who have pity on the poor, lend to You, LORD; and that which I have given, You will pay me again.

Proverbs 19:17

If I turn again to You, LORD, my brothers and my children shall find compassion . . . for You, the LORD my God, are gracious and merciful, and will not turn away Your face from me, if I return to You.

2 Chronicles 30:9

Compassion

"When you make a dinner or supper, do not call your friends, nor your brothers, neither your relatives nor your rich neighbors, lest they also invite you again, and a recompense be made you. But when you make a feast, call the poor, the maimed, the lame, the blind, and you will be blessed, for they cannot repay you. For you shall be repaid at the resurrection of the just."

Luke 14:12-14

God, You are not unrighteous to forget my work and labor of love which I have shown toward Your name, in that I have ministered and continue to minister.

Hebrews 6:10

If I can stop one heart from breaking,
I shall not live in vain;
If I can ease one life the aching,
Or cool one pain,
Or help one fainting robin
Unto his nest again,
I shall not live in vain.

Emily Elizabeth Dickinson

A CHRIST-LIKE HEART REFLECTS GOD'S . . .

COURAGE

The exceeding greatness of Your power is to me who believes, according to the working of Your mighty power, which You wrought in Christ when You raised Him from the dead.

Ephesians 1:19-20

Praise You, LORD. I am blessed who fear You, who delight greatly in Your commandments. My seed shall be mighty upon the earth. My generation, the generation of the upright, shall be blessed.

Psalm 112:1-2

"Deal courageously, and I, the LORD, shall be with the good."

2 Chronicles 19:11

The weapons of my warfare are not carnal, but mighty through You, God, to the pulling down of strongholds; I cast down imaginations and every high thing that exalts itself against the knowledge of You, God, and bring every thought into captivity to the obedience of Christ.

2 Corinthians 10:4-5

My defense is from You, God, who saves the upright in heart.

Psalm 7:10

COURAGE

Light arises to me, the upright, in the darkness. . . . I am not afraid of evil tidings; my heart is fixed, trusting in You, LORD.

Psalm 112:4,7

"These things I have spoken to you, that in Me you might have peace. In the world you will have tribulation, but be of good cheer, I have overcome the world."

John 16:33

God, You have not given me the spirit of fear, but of power, and of love, and of a sound mind.

2 Timothy 1:7

"Wait on Me, your LORD. Be of good courage, and I shall strengthen your heart. Wait, I say, on Me."

Psalm 27:14

"Be strong and very courageous, that you may observe to do according to all My law . . . and do not turn from it to the right hand or to the left, that you may prosper wherever you go."

Joshua 1:7

Courage

Through You, God, I shall do valiantly, for You shall tread down my enemies.

Psalm 60:12

Your truth shall be my shield and buckler. . . . I will not be afraid of the terror at night, nor for the arrow that flies by day, nor for the plague that walks in darkness, nor for the destruction that wastes at noon.

Psalm 91:4-6

LORD, You are on my side; I will not fear. What can man do to me? You are for me along with those who help me, therefore I shall see my desire upon those who hate me. It is better to trust in You than to put confidence in man.

Psalm 118:6-9

I am strong and of good courage; I do not fear, nor am I afraid of them, for You, LORD my God, go with me; You will not fail me, nor forsake me.

Deuteronomy 31:6

Have plenty of courage. God is stronger than the devil. We are on the winning side.

John Jay Chapman

A CHRIST-LIKE HEART REFLECTS GOD'S . . .

ENCOURAGEMENT

The liberal soul shall be made prosperous, and I who water shall be watered also myself.

Proverbs 11:25

Pleasant words are as a honeycomb, sweet to the soul, and health to the bones.

Proverbs 16:24

A word fitly spoken [by me] is like apples of gold in pictures of silver.

Proverbs 25:11

LORD my God, You are He who goes with me, to fight for me against my enemies, to save me.

Deuteronomy 20:4

Blessed are You, LORD, who have given rest to Your people Israel, according to all that You promised. Not one word has failed of all Your good promise, which You promised by the hand of Moses Your servant.

1 Kings 8:56

Do not rejoice against me, O my enemy; when I fall, I shall arise; when I sit in darkness, the LORD shall be a light to me.

Micah 7:8

ENCOURAGEMENT

You, the Lord GOD, have given me the tongue of the learned, that I should know how to speak a word in season to him who is weary.

Isaiah 50:4

LORD, You are near to all who call upon You, to all who call upon You in truth. You will fulfill the desire of those [like me] who fear You. You also will hear our cry and will save us.

Psalm 145:18-19

God, You are more abundantly willing to show to the heirs of promise the unchangeability of Your counsel; You confirmed it by an oath, that by two unchangeable things, in which it was impossible for You to lie, I might have a strong consolation.

Hebrews 6:17-18

Kindness is a language which the deaf can hear and the blind can see.

Mark Twain

FAITH

God, You have dealt to me, and everyone, the measure of faith.

Romans 12:3

"Trust in Me, your LORD, with all your heart; and lean not on your own understanding. In all your ways, acknowledge Me, and I will direct your paths."

Proverbs 3:5-6

[Paul's] speech and his preaching were not with enticing words of man's wisdom but in demonstration of Your Spirit and of power, that my faith should not stand in the wisdom of men but in Your power, God.

1 Corinthians 2:4-5

"Have faith in God. . . . Whatever things you desire, when you pray, believe that you receive them, and you shall have them."

Mark 11:22,24

The effectual fervent prayer of the righteous avails much.

James 5:16

My faith comes by hearing, and hearing by Your word, God.

Romans 10:17

FAITH

I am crucified with Christ, nevertheless I live; yet not I, but Christ lives in me. And the life which I now live in the flesh, I live by the faith of the Son of God, who loved me and gave Himself for me.

Galatians 2:20

Above all, I am taking the shield of faith, with which I shall be able to quench all the fiery darts of the wicked.

Ephesians 6:16

By grace I am saved through faith, and that not of myself; it is Your gift, God.

Ephesians 2:8

Jesus Christ, whom having not seen, I love; in whom, though now I do not see Him, yet believing, I rejoice with joy unspeakable and full of glory, receiving the end of my faith, even the salvation of my soul.

1 Peter 1:7-9

FAITH

"If you have faith as a grain of mustard seed, you shall say to this mountain, 'Remove from here to yonder place,' and it shall move; and nothing shall be impossible to you."

Matthew 17:20

"Whatever you shall ask of the Father, in My name, I will give it to you. . . . Ask and you shall receive, that your joy may be full."

John 16:23-24

Without faith it is impossible to please You, for the one who comes to You must believe that You are and that You are a rewarder of those who diligently seek You.

Hebrews 11:6

"The ones who believe on Me, the works that I do shall they do also, and greater works than these shall they do, because I go to My Father."

John 14:12

The just shall live by their faith.

Habakkuk 2:4

FAITH

Jesus said to him, "If you can believe, all things are possible to the one who believes."

And right away the father of the child cried out, and said with tears, "Lord, I believe; help my unbelief."

Mark 9:23-24

Whatever is born of You, God, overcomes the world; and this is the victory that overcomes the world, even my faith.

1 John 5:4

Now Your righteousness, God, without the law is manifested, being witnessed by the law and the prophets; even Your righteousness which is by faith in Jesus Christ to all and upon all those who believe, for there is no difference.

Romans 3:21-22

Faith is not believing that God can, but that God will!

Abraham Lincoln

A Christ-like Heart Reflects God's . . .

Forgiveness

"Judge not, and you shall not be judged. Condemn not, and you shall not be condemned. Forgive, and you shall be forgiven."

Luke 6:37

Great peace I have who love Your law, and nothing shall offend me.

Psalm 119:165

"Confess your faults to one another and pray for one another, that you may be healed."

James 5:16

Giving thanks to You, Father, who has . . . translated me into the kingdom of Your dear Son, in whom I have redemption through His blood, even the forgiveness of sins.

Colossians 1:12-14

I, being dead in my sins . . . You have quickened together with Jesus, having forgiven me all offenses, blotting out the note of debt that was against me, which was antagonistic to me. You took it out of the way, nailing it to Jesus' cross.

Colossians 2:13-14

Forgiveness

"When you stand praying, forgive if you have anything against anyone, that your Father also who is in heaven, may forgive you your offenses."

Mark 11:25

"I, the Son of man, have power on earth to forgive your sins."

Luke 5:24

"Be it known to you therefore, . . . that through this Man is preached to you the forgiveness of sins. And by Him all who believe are justified from all things, from which you could not be justified by the law of Moses."

Acts 13:38-39

I have redemption through His blood, the forgiveness of sins, according to the riches of His grace.

Ephesians 1:7

"If you forgive others their offenses, your heavenly Father will also forgive you."

Matthew 6:14

Blessed am I whose offenses are forgiven and whose sins are covered. Blessed am I to whom the Lord will not impute sin.

Romans 4:7

FORGIVENESS

"Put on . . . longsuffering, bearing with one another and forgiving one another if anyone has a quarrel against anyone. Even as Christ forgave you, so also are you to forgive."

Colossians 3:12-13

As far as the east is from the west, so far have You removed my transgressions from me.

Psalm 103:12

"'Come now, and let us reason together,' says the LORD. 'Though your sins are as scarlet, they shall be as white as snow. Though they are red like crimson, they shall be as wool.'"

Isaiah 1:18

"I am He who blots out your transgressions for My own sake and will not remember your sins. Put Me in remembrance; let us plead together. Speak, that you may be justified."

Isaiah 43:25-26

It is cheaper to pardon than to resent. Forgiveness saves the expense of anger, the cost of hatred.

Hannah More

FREEDOM

I look into the perfect law of liberty, and continue in it, not being a forgetful hearer, but a doer of the work, I shall be blessed in my deed.

James 1:25

I have been called to liberty, only I am not to use liberty for an occasion to indulge the flesh, but by love I am to serve others.

Galatians 5:13

"Stand fast in the liberty with which Christ has made us free, and do not be entangled again with the yoke of bondage."

Galatians 5:1

The law of the Spirit of life in Christ Jesus has made me free from the law of sin and death.

Romans 8:2

"The Spirit of the Lord is upon Me, because He has anointed Me . . . to set at liberty those who are bruised."

Luke 4:18

FREEDOM

I will walk at liberty, for I seek Your precepts.

Psalm 119:45

Restore to me the joy of Your salvation, and uphold me with Your free Spirit. Then will I teach transgressors Your ways, and sinners shall be converted to You.

Psalm 51:12-13

You shall know the truth, and the truth will make you free.

John 8:32

"If I, the Son, shall make you free, you shall be free indeed."

John 8:36

I, who was baptized into Jesus Christ, was baptized into His death; therefore, I am buried with Him by baptism into death. Likewise, as Christ was raised up from the dead by the glory of the Father, even so I also should walk in newness of life . . . knowing this, that my old man is crucified with Him, that the body of sin might be destroyed, that from now on I should not serve sin. For the one who is dead is freed from sin.

Romans 6:3-4,6-7

FREEDOM

Where the Spirit of the Lord is, there is liberty [for me].

2 Corinthians 3:17

Though I am free from all men, yet I have made myself servant to all, that I might gain more.

1 Corinthians 9:19

Being made free from sin, I became the servant of righteousness.

Romans 6:18

"Take heed lest by any means this liberty of mine become a stumbling block to those who are weak."

1 Corinthians 8:9

He that is good is free, though he is a slave;
he that is evil is a slave, though he be a king.

Augustine of Hippo

A Christ-like Heart Reflects God's . . .

Friendship

I make no friendship with an angry man, and with a furious man I shall not go, lest I learn his ways and get a snare to my soul.

Proverbs 22:24

The one who has friends must show himself friendly, and there is a friend who sticks closer than a brother.

Proverbs 18:24

The one who loves pureness of heart, for the grace of his lips the king shall be his friend.

Proverbs 22:11

A friend loves at all times, and a brother is born for adversity.

Proverbs 17:17

Friendship of the world is enmity with You, God. Whoever therefore would be a friend of the world is Your enemy.

James 4:4

Abraham believed You, and it was imputed to him for righteousness, and he was called Your Friend, God.

James 2:23

FRIENDSHIP

Iron sharpens iron, so a man sharpens the countenance of his friend.

Proverbs 27:17

"Your own friend and your father's friend, do not forsake; neither go into your brother's house in the day of your calamity. Better is a neighbor who is near than a brother far off."

Proverbs 27:10

Faithful are the wounds of a friend, but the kisses of an enemy are deceitful.

Proverbs 27:6

LORD, who shall abide in Your tabernacle? Who shall dwell in Your holy hill? He who walks uprightly and works righteousness and speaks the truth in his heart. He who doesn't backbite with his tongue, nor takes up a reproach against his neighbor.

Psalm 15:1-3

"From now on I do not call you servants, for the servant does not know what his lord does, but I have called you friends, for all things that I have heard of My Father I have made known to you."

John 15:15

What is a friend? A single soul dwelling in two bodies.

Aristotle

A Christ-like Heart Reflects God's . . .

Generosity

"Give and it will be given to you—good measure, pressed down, shaken together, and running over, will men give to you. For with the same measure that you use, it shall be measured to you as well."

Luke 6:38

"Honor Me, Your LORD, with your substance and with the first of all your increase, so your barns will be filled with plenty and your presses will burst out with new wine."

Proverbs 3:9-10

"'Bring all your tithes into the storehouse, that there may be meat in My house. And prove Me now by this,' says the Lord of hosts, 'if I will open to you the windows of heaven and pour you out a blessing, that there will not be room enough to receive it. And I will rebuke the devourer for your sake.'"

Malachi 3:10-11

Generosity

The one who has a bountiful eye shall be blessed, for he gives of his bread to the poor.

Proverbs 22:9

The one who sows sparingly shall also reap sparingly, and the one who sows bountifully shall also reap bountifully. Everyone according as they purpose in their heart so let them give, not grudgingly or of necessity; for, God, You love a cheerful giver. And You are able to make all grace abound toward me, so that I, always having all sufficiency in all things, may abound to every good work.

2 Corinthians 9:6-8

"Trust in Me, your LORD, and do good, so you shall dwell in the land, and truly you shall be fed."

Psalm 37:3

"To you who knows to do good and does not do it, to you it is sin."

James 4:17

Do all the good you can, to all the people you can, in all the ways you can, as often as ever you can, as long as you can.

Charles Haddon Spurgeon

A Christ-like Heart Reflects God's . . .

Hope

Now the God of hope fill me with all joy and peace in believing, that I may abound in hope through the power of the Holy Spirit.

Romans 15:13

Whatever things were written before were written for my learning, that I through patience and comfort of the scriptures might have hope.

Romans 15:4

The mystery, which has been hidden from ages and from generations but now is made manifest to Your saints, . . . is Christ in us, the hope of glory.

Colossians 1:26-27

If in this life only, we have hope in Christ, we are of all men most miserable. But now Christ is risen from the dead.

1 Corinthians 15:19-20

Remember the word to Your servant upon which You have caused me to hope. This is my comfort in my affliction, for Your word has revived me.

Psalm 119:49-50

Hope

Your eye, LORD, is upon me who fears You, upon me who hopes in Your mercy, to deliver my soul from death and to keep me alive in famine.

Psalm 33:18-19

"The LORD is my portion," says my soul, "therefore I will hope in Him." You, LORD, are good to me who waits for You, to the soul who seeks You. It is good that I should both hope and quietly wait for Your salvation, LORD.

Lamentations 3:24-26

In You, LORD, do I hope; You will hear, O Lord my God.

Psalm 38:15

Being justified by Your grace, I should be made an heir according to the hope of eternal life.

Titus 3:7

My soul waits for You, LORD. You are my help and my shield. For my heart will rejoice in You because I have trusted in Your holy name. Let Your mercy, O LORD, be upon me, according as I hope in You.

Psalm 33:20-22

Hope

By [my Lord Jesus Christ] I also have access by faith into this grace in which I stand, and I rejoice in hope of the glory of God.

Romans 5:2

You are my hope, O Lord GOD. You are my trust from my youth. . . . I will hope continually and will yet praise You more and more.

Psalm 71:5,14

I am saved by hope, but hope that is seen is not hope. For if one sees, why does he yet hope for it? But if I hope for that which I do not see, then I do patiently wait for it.

Romans 8:24-25

Paul wrote: We heard of your faith in Christ Jesus and of the love that you have for all the saints because of the hope which is laid up for you in heaven.

Colossians 1:4-5

HOPE

More abundantly willing to show to the heirs of promise [and to me], the unchangeability of Your counsel, You confirmed it by an oath, that by two unchangeable things, in which it was impossible for You to lie, I, who have fled for refuge, might have a strong consolation to lay hold upon the hope set before me, which hope I have as an anchor of my soul, both sure and steadfast.

Hebrews 6:17-19

I have set You, LORD, always before me; because You are at my right hand, I shall not be moved. Therefore my heart is glad, and my glory rejoices; my flesh also shall rest in hope.

Psalm 16:8-9

Why are you cast down, O my soul? And why are you disquieted within me? Hope in God. I shall yet praise You who are the health of my countenance and my God.

Psalm 42:11

Hope

Those who fear You will be glad when they see me, because I have hoped in Your word.

Psalm 119:74

As the sufferings of Christ abound in me, so my consolation also abounds by Christ.

2 Corinthians 1:5

I was without Christ, an alien from the commonwealth of Israel and a stranger from the covenants of promise, having no hope and without God, in the world. But now in Christ Jesus, I, who sometimes was far off, am made near by the blood of Christ.

Ephesians 2:12-13

'Tis always morning somewhere.

Henry Wadsworth Longfellow

A CHRIST-LIKE HEART REFLECTS GOD'S . . .

INTEGRITY

The LORD shall judge the people; judge me, O LORD, according to my righteousness and according to my integrity that is in me. Oh let the wickedness of the wicked come to an end, but establish the just, for You, the righteous God, try the minds and hearts. My defense is of God, who saves the upright in heart.

Psalm 7:8-10

I who speak truth show forth righteousness. . . . Lying lips are an abomination to You, LORD, but I who deal truly am Your delight.

Proverbs 12:17,22

Your word, LORD, is right, and all Your works are done in truth. You love righteousness and judgment. The earth is full of Your goodness, LORD.

Psalm 33:4-5

The mouth of the just brings forth wisdom, but the perverse tongue shall be cut out.

Proverbs 10:31

Integrity

You are the Rock, Your work is perfect, for all Your ways are judgment; a God of truth and without evildoing, just and right are You.

Deuteronomy 32:4

You shall cover me with Your feathers, and under Your wings I shall trust. Your truth shall be my shield and buckler.

Psalm 91:4

Behold, You desire truth in the inward parts, and in the hidden part You shall make me to know wisdom.

Psalm 51:6

I who walk uprightly, walk surely, but the one who perverts his ways shall be known.

Proverbs 10:9

The integrity of the upright will guide them, but the perverseness of transgressors will destroy them.

Proverbs 11:3

Righteousness keeps me who is upright in the way, but wickedness overthrows the sinner.

Proverbs 13:6

Always do right. This will gratify some people and astonish the rest.

Mark Twain

JOY

[I am] looking to Jesus, the author and finisher of my faith; who for the joy that was set before Him endured the cross, despising the shame, and is set down at the right hand of Your throne, God.

Hebrews 12:2

You have turned for me my mourning into dancing. You have put off my sackcloth, and girded me with gladness to the end that my glory may sing praise to You, and not be silent.

Psalm 30:11-12

"If you keep My commandments, you shall abide in My love; even as I have kept My Father's commandments and abide in His love. These things I have spoken to you that My joy might remain in you and that your joy might be full."

John 15:10-11

A merry heart [even mine] does good like a medicine, but a broken spirit dries the bones.

Proverbs 17:22

Your joy, LORD, is my strength.

Nehemiah 8:10

JOY

A merry heart [even mine] makes a cheerful countenance, but by sorrow of the heart the spirit is broken.

Proverbs 15:13

All the days of the afflicted are evil, but I who am of a merry heart have a continual feast.

Proverbs 15:15

I shall go out with joy and be led forth with peace. The mountains and the hills shall break forth before me into singing, and all the trees of the field shall clap their hands.

Isaiah 55:12

Your kingdom, God, is not meat and drink, but righteousness, and peace, and joy in the Holy Spirit.

Romans 14:17

You will show me the path of life. In Your presence is fullness of joy. At Your right hand there are pleasures forevermore.

Psalm 16:11

For the Heart
That finds joy
In small things
Each day is
A wonderful gift.

Unknown

A Christ-like Heart Reflects God's . . .

Kindness

How excellent is Your lovingkindness, O God! Therefore the children of men put their trust under the shadow of Your wings. . . . O continue Your lovingkindness to me, who knows You, and Your righteousness to [me,] the upright in heart.

Psalm 36:7,10

He is kind to the unthankful and to the evil. Therefore, you be merciful, as your Father also is merciful.

Luke 6:35-36

After that, the kindness and love of God my Savior to me appeared, not by works of righteousness which I have done, but according to His mercy He saved me, by the washing of regeneration and renewing of the Holy Spirit.

Titus 3:4-5

You, God, for Christ's sake have forgiven me.

Ephesians 4:32

Hear me, O LORD; for Your lovingkindess is good. Turn to me according to the multitude of Your tender mercies.

Psalm 69:16

A Christ-like Heart Reflects God's . . .

Kindness

"'With everlasting kindness I will have mercy on you,' says the LORD your Redeemer."

Isaiah 54:8

Show Your marvelous lovingkindness, O You who save by Your right hand those who put their trust in You from those who rise up against them.

Psalm 17:7

Because Your lovingkindness is better than life, my lips shall praise You.

Psalm 63:3

I will worship toward Your holy temple and praise Your name for Your lovingkindness and for Your truth, for You have magnified Your word above all Your name.

Psalm 138:2

You are a God ready to pardon, gracious and merciful, slow to anger, and of great kindness, and You did not forsake me.

Nehemiah 9:17

Love suffers long and is kind.

1 Corinthians 13:4

"I am the LORD who exercises lovingkindness, judgment, and righteousness, in the earth, for in these things I delight."

Jeremiah 9:24

Kindness

God, You are love.

1 John 4:16

The merciful person does good to their own soul, but the one who is cruel troubles their own flesh.

Proverbs 11:17

Your merciful kindness is great toward me, and Your truth, LORD, endures forever. Praise You, LORD.

Psalm 117:2

Let Your merciful kindness be for my comfort, according to Your word to Your servant.

Psalm 119:76

You, LORD, will command Your lovingkindness in the daytime, and in the night Your song shall be with me, and my prayer to You, the God of my life.

Psalm 42:8

Blessed are You, LORD, for You have shown me Your marvelous kindness in a strong city. . . . You heard the voice of my supplications when I cried to You.

Psalm 31:21-22

Little drops of water, little grains of sand,
Make the mighty ocean and the pleasant land.
Little deeds of kindness, little words of love,
Help to make earth happy like the heaven above.

Julia A. Fletcher Carney

A CHRIST-LIKE HEART REFLECTS GOD'S . . .

LAUGHTER

LORD, when You turned again the captivity of Zion, we were like those who dream. Then our mouth was filled with laughter and our tongue with singing. Then they said among the nations, "The LORD has done great things for them." You, LORD, have done great things for us, for which we are glad.

Psalm 126:21-3

To everything there is a season, and a time to every purpose under the heaven . . . a time to weep, and a time to laugh; a time to mourn, and a time to dance.

Ecclesiastes 3:1,4

"Blessed are you who weep now, for you shall laugh."

Luke 6:21

Rejoice, O young person in your youth, and let your heart cheer you in the days of your youth, and walk in the ways of your heart, and in the sight of your eyes

Ecclesiastes 11:9

Laughter lightens the load!

Maria Thusick

A Christ-like Heart Reflects God's . . .

Love

Love is long suffering and kind; it does not envy . . . it is not puffed up, it does not behave itself unbecomingly, it does not seek its own way, is not easily provoked, thinks no evil; it does not rejoice in evildoing but rejoices in the truth; it bears all things, believes all things, hopes all things, endures all things. Love never fails.

1 Corinthians 13:4-8

"Love your enemies and do good and lend, hoping for nothing in return; and your reward will be great, and you shall be the children of the Highest; for He is kind to the unthankful and to the evil."

Luke 6:35

Hatred stirs up strife, but love covers all sins.

Proverbs 10:12

I know that I have passed from death to life, because I love the brethren.

1 John 3:14

Love

I love Him, because He first loved me.

1 John 4:19

I am persuaded that neither death, nor life, nor angels, nor principalities, nor powers, nor things present, nor things to come, nor height, nor depth, nor any other creature, will be able to separate me from Your love, God, which is in Christ Jesus my Lord.

Romans 8:38-39

"A new commandment I give to you, that you love one another. As I have loved you, you also love one another. By this shall all men know that you are My disciples, if you have love one to another."

John 13:34-35

The one who does not love, does not know God; for You, God, are love.

1 John 4:8

God, You are rich in mercy. Because of Your great love with which You loved us, even when we was dead in sins, You have made us alive together with Christ (by grace we are saved).

Ephesians 2:4-5

Love

I perceive Your love, God, because You laid down Your life for me. And I ought to lay down my life for my brothers and sisters in Christ.

1 John 3:16

"Above all these things put on love, which is the bond of perfection."

Colossians 3:14

"Thus says the LORD, 'Yes, I have loved you with an everlasting love, therefore with lovingkindness I have drawn you.'"

Jeremiah 31:3

Let us love one another, for love is of God, and everyone who loves is born of God and knows God.

1 John 4:7

Hope does not make ashamed, because Your love, God, is shed abroad in my heart by the Holy Spirit, who is given to me.

Romans 5:5

God, You loved us so much that You gave Your only begotten Son, that I, who believe in Him, shall not perish but will have everlasting life.

John 3:16

LOVE

I have known and believed the love that You, God, have for me. You are love; and I who dwell in love, dwell in You, and You dwell in me.

1 John 4:16

When we were yet without strength, in due time Christ died for the ungodly. One will scarcely die for a righteous man, yet perhaps for a good man some would even dare to die. But You, God, commend Your love toward me, in that while I was yet a sinner, Christ died for me.

Romans 5:6-8

May [I] be able to comprehend with all saints what is the breadth, and length, and depth, and height; and to know the love of Christ which passes knowledge, that I might be filled with all Your fullness, God.

Ephesians 3:18-20

Our Lord does not care so much for the importance of our works as for the love with which they are done.

Teresa of Avila

LOYALTY

A talebearer reveals secrets, but the one who is of a faithful spirit conceals the matter.

Proverbs 11:13

You honor those who fear You, LORD, one who swears to his own hurt and does not change.

Psalm 15:4

A friend loves at all times, and a brother is born for adversity.

Proverbs 17:17

"No one has greater love than this, that one lay down his life for his friends."

John 15:13

A faithful witness will not lie, but a false witness will utter lies.

Proverbs 14:5

[Love] thinks no evil, does not rejoice in evildoing, but rejoices in the truth; bears all things, believes all things, hopes all things, endures all things. [Love] never fails.

1 Corinthians 13:5-8

I will speak ill of no man and speak all the good I know of everybody.

Benjamin Franklin

A CHRIST-LIKE HEART REFLECTS GOD'S . . .

MERCY

Not by works of righteousness which I have done, but according to Your mercy You saved me, by the washing of regeneration and renewing of the Holy Spirit.

Titus 3:5

I have a great high priest . . . Jesus the Son of God. . . . I do not have a high priest who cannot be touched with the feeling of my infirmities. . . . Let me, therefore, come boldly to the throne of grace, that I may obtain mercy and find grace to help in time of need.

Hebrews 4:14-16

Blessed are You, the God and Father of my Lord Jesus Christ, who according to Your abundant mercy have begotten me again to a lively hope by the resurrection of Jesus Christ from the dead.

1 Peter 1:3

By mercy and truth, evildoing is purged.

Proverbs 16:6

MERCY

Blessed are the merciful, for they shall obtain mercy.

Matthew 5:7

Through Your tender mercy, God, the dayspring from on high has visited me, to give light to me who sits in darkness and in the shadow of death, to guide my feet into the way of peace.

Luke 1:78-79

Mercy and truth preserve the king, and his throne is upheld by mercy.

Proverbs 20:28

I will not hunger nor thirst, nor will the heat nor the sun smite me, for You who have mercy on me will lead me, even by the springs of water will You guide me.

Isaiah 49:10

"Sow to yourselves in righteousness, reap in mercy; break up your fallow ground, for it is time to seek the LORD, till He come and rain righteousness upon you."

Hosea 10:12

The one who despises their neighbor sins, but if I have mercy on the poor I am happy.

Proverbs 14:21

MERCY

"Do not let mercy and truth forsake you. Bind them about your neck; write them upon the table of your heart, so shall you find favor and good understanding in the sight of God and man."

Proverbs 3:3-4

Let me return to You, LORD, and You will have mercy on me; and to You, God, for You will abundantly pardon.

Isaiah 55:7

"Turn to Me, your God; keep mercy and judgment, and wait on Me continually."

Hosea 12:6

"Be merciful, as your Father, also is merciful. Judge not, and you shall not be judged. Condemn not, and you shall not be condemned. Forgive, and you shall be forgiven."

Luke 6:36-37

LORD, You are merciful and gracious, slow to anger and plenteous in mercy.

Psalm 103:8

I who follow after righteousness and mercy find life, righteousness, and honor.

Proverbs 21:21

MERCY

O LORD God of heaven, the great and terrible God, who keeps covenant and mercy for me who loves You and observes Your commandments, let Your ear now be attentive and Your eyes open.

Nehemiah 1:5-6

O LORD God of Israel, there is no God like You in the heaven, nor in the earth who keeps covenant and shows mercy to Your servants, who walk before You with all their hearts.

2 Chronicles 6:14

Your mercy is on those who fear You, from generation to generation.

Luke 1:50

You have shown me . . . what is good; and what do You, LORD, require of me but to do justly and to love mercy and to walk humbly with You, my God?

Micah 6:8

Remember, O LORD, Your tender mercies and Your loving kindnesses, for they have been ever of old.

Psalm 25:6

Mercy imitates God and disappoints Satan.

Saint John Chrysostom

A Christ-like Heart Reflects God's . . .

Obedience

"Servants, [employees,] obey in all things your masters [employers] according to the flesh, not with eye-service as people pleasers, but in singleness of heart, fearing God. And whatever you do, do it heartily as to the Lord and not to men, knowing that of the Lord you shall receive the reward of the inheritance, for you serve the Lord Christ."

Colossians 3:22-24

"Obey those who have the rule over you, and submit yourselves, (for they watch for your souls, as those who must give account), that they may do it with joy and not with grief, for that is unprofitable for you."

Hebrews 13:17

Being made perfect, [Jesus] became the author of eternal salvation to all who obey Him.

Hebrews 5:9

"Children obey your parents in all things, for this is well pleasing to the Me, your Lord."

Colossians 3:20

Obedience

"The one who has My commandments, and keeps them, he is the one who loves Me. And the one who loves Me shall be loved of My Father, and I will love him, and will manifest Myself to him."

John 14:21

"Whatever you ask, you receive of Me, because you keep My commandments and do those things that are pleasing in My sight."

1 John 3:22

"Seeing you have purified your souls in obeying the truth through the Spirit to sincere love of the believers, see that you love one another with a pure heart fervently."

1 Peter 1:22

"Children, obey your parents in the Lord, for this is right. Honor your father and mother, (which is the first commandment with promise;) that it may be well with you, and you may live long on the earth."

Ephesians 6:1-3

OBEDIENCE

By this do I know that I know You, if I keep Your commandments, God. If I say I know You, and do not keep Your commandments, I am a liar, and the truth is not in me.

1 John 2:3-4

"If you keep My commandments, you shall abide in My love; even as I have kept My Father's commandments, and abide in His love."

John 15:10

"Don't you know that to whomever you yield yourselves as servants to obey, you are servants of the one you obey, whether of sin to death, or of obedience to righteousness?"

Romans 6:16

"Whoever shall do the will of My Father who is in heaven, the same is My brother, and sister, and mother."

Matthew 12:50

"To obey is better than sacrifice."

1 Samuel 15:22

Thirty years of our Lord's life are hidden in these words of the gospel: "He was subject unto them."

Jacques Bénigne Bossuet

PATIENCE

I have need of patience so that after I have done Your will, God, I might receive the promise.

Hebrews 10:36

"I am not slack concerning My promise, as some men count slackness, but I am patient with you, not willing that you or any should perish, but that all should come to repentance."

2 Peter 3:9

Whatever things were written before were written for my learning, that I through patience and comfort of the scriptures might have hope.

Romans 15:4

Knowing this, the trying of my faith works patience. Let patience have her perfect work, that I may be perfect and entire, lacking nothing.

James 1:3-4

Seeing that I am surrounded by so great a cloud of witnesses, I lay aside every weight and the sin that so easily harasses me. I run with patience the race that You set before me, looking to Jesus, the author and finisher of my faith.

Hebrews 12:1-2

PATIENCE

It is good that I should both hope and quietly wait for Your salvation, LORD.

Lamentations 3:26

"Be patient for the coming of the Lord. The farmer waits for the precious fruit of the earth, and has long patience for it, until he receives the early and latter rain. You also be patient; establish your heart, for the coming of the Lord draws near."

James 5:7-8

I glory in tribulations, knowing that tribulation develops patience.

Romans 5:3

I waited patiently for You, LORD, and You listened to me and heard my cry.

Psalm 40:1

"Show the same diligence to the full assurance of hope to the end. Be not lazy, but followers of those who through faith and patience inherit the promises."

Hebrews 6:11-12

Let nothing disturb you.Let nothing affright you.
All things are passing. God never changes.
Patience gains all things.
Whoever has God wants nothing.God alone suffices.

Teresa of Avila

A Christ-like Heart Reflects God's . . .

Peace

You have delivered my soul in peace from the battle that was against me, for there were many with me.

Psalm 55:18

All things are of You, God, who have reconciled me to Yourself by Jesus Christ and have given to me the ministry of reconciliation. To wit, that You were in Christ, reconciling me to Yourself, not counting my sins against me, and You have committed to me the word of reconciliation.

2 Corinthians 5:18-19

"Peace I leave with you, my peace I give to you, not as the world gives do I give to you. Do not let your heart be troubled, neither let it be afraid."

John 14:27

LORD, You are my shepherd. I shall not want. You make me to lie down in green pastures. You lead me beside the still waters.

Psalm 23:1-2

PEACE

Great peace have I who love Your law, and nothing shall offend me.

Psalm 119:165

If when we were enemies, I was reconciled to You,God, by the death of Your Son, much more, being reconciled, I shall be saved by His life.

Romans 5:10

"Be still and know that I am God. I will be exalted among the unbelievers; I will be exalted in the earth."

Psalm 46:10

"The work of righteousness shall be peace, and the effect of righteousness quietness and assurance forever. And My people shall dwell in a peaceable habitation and in sure dwellings, and in quiet resting places."

Isaiah 32:17-18

"Don't worry about anything, but in everything by prayer and supplication with thanksgiving, let your requests be made known to Me. And My peace, which passes all understanding, will keep your heart and mind through Christ Jesus."

Philippians 4:6-7

Peace

"'The mountains will depart, and the hills be removed, but My kindness will not depart from you, neither will the covenant of My peace be removed,' says the LORD who has mercy on you."

Isaiah 54:10

The punishment for my peace was upon Him [Jesus].

Isaiah 53:5

Mark the perfect man and behold the upright, for the end of that man shall be peace.

Psalm 37:37

"Do those things, which you have both learned, and received, and heard and seen in me [the apostle Paul], and the God of peace will be with you."

Philippians 4:9

Being justified by faith, we have peace with You, God, through our Lord Jesus Christ.

Romans 5:1

To be carnally minded is death, but to be spiritually minded is life and peace.

Romans 8:6

PEACE

God is not the author of confusion, but of peace, as in all churches of the saints.

1 Corinthians 14:33

"Blessed are the peacemakers, for they shall be called children of God."

Matthew 5:9

Deceit is in the heart of those who imagine evil, but to the counselors of peace is joy.

Proverbs 12:20

You will keep me in perfect peace, whose mind is stayed on You, because I trust in You.

Isaiah 26:3

"'I create the fruit of the lips. Peace, peace to the one who is far off and to you who are near, and I will heal you,' says the LORD."

Isaiah 57:19

The fruit of righteousness is sown in peace by me, who makes peace.

James 3:18

First keep the peace within yourself,
then you can also bring peace to others.

Thomas à Kempis

A CHRIST-LIKE HEART REFLECTS GOD'S . . .

PERSEVERANCE

"Stand fast, therefore, in the liberty with which Christ has made you free, and do not be entangled again with the yoke of bondage."

Galatians 5:1

James said, "We count them happy who endure. You have heard of the patience of Job, and have seen the end of the Lord; that the Lord is very compassionate, and of tender mercy."

James 5:11

"Stand fast and hold the traditions that you have been taught, whether by word or by the epistles. Now your Lord Jesus Christ Himself and God, even your Father, who has loved you and has given you everlasting consolation and good hope through grace, comfort your heart and establish you in every good word and work."

2 Thessalonians 2:15-17

I am made a partaker of Christ, if I hold the beginning of my confidence steadfast until the end.

Hebrews 3:14

PERSEVERANCE

"You be steadfast, immovable, always abounding in the work of the Lord, inasmuch as you know that your labor is not in vain in the Lord."

1 Corinthians 15:58

Lord God, You will help me, therefore I will not be disgraced; I have set my face like a flint, and I know that I shall not be ashamed.

Isaiah 50:7

"Be strong and do not let your hands become weak, for your work shall be rewarded."

2 Chronicles 15:7

Save me, O God, by Your name, and judge me by Your strength. Hear my prayer, O God; give ear to the words of my mouth. Strangers have risen up against me, and oppressors seek after my soul. They have not set You before them. Behold, You are my helper. You are with those who uphold my soul.

Psalm 54:1-4

PERSEVERANCE

"Wait on Me, your LORD. Be of good courage, and I will strengthen your heart. Wait, I say, on Me, your LORD."

Psalm 27:14

Lord GOD, You will help me, therefore I will not be disgraced; I have set my face like a flint, and I know that I shall not be ashamed.

Isaiah 50:7

I am troubled on every side, yet not distressed; I am perplexed, but not in despair; persecuted, but not forsaken; cast down, but not destroyed; always bearing about in my body the dying of the Lord Jesus, that the life also of Jesus might be made manifest in my body.

2 Corinthians 4:8-10

Every oak tree started out as a couple of nuts who stood their ground.

Unknown

A Christ-like Heart Reflects God's . . .

Prayer

Building myself up on my most holy faith, praying in the Holy Spirit.

Jude 20

The effectual fervent prayer of a righteous person avails much.

James 5:16

If I pray in an unknown tongue, my spirit prays, but my understanding is unfruitful. . . . I will pray with the spirit, and I will pray with the understanding also.

1 Corinthians 14:14-15

[The apostle Paul wrote,] "I exhort therefore, that, first of all, supplications, prayers, intercessions, and giving of thanks, be made for all men, for kings [government leaders], and for all who are in authority, that we may lead a quiet and peaceable life in all godliness and honesty. For this is good and acceptable in the sight of God our Savior, who will have all people to be saved, and to come to the knowledge of the truth."

1 Timothy 2:1-4

PRAYER

Your eyes, Lord, are over the righteous, and Your ears are open to their prayers.

1 Peter 3:12

"The end of all things is at hand, be therefore sober, and watch for the purpose of prayer."

1 Peter 4:7

"Be anxious for nothing, but in everything by prayer and supplication with thanksgiving, let your requests be made known to Me, your God. And My peace, which passes all understanding, shall keep your hearts and minds through Christ Jesus."

Philippians 4:6-7

The Spirit also helps my infirmities, for I do not know what I should pray for as I ought, but the Spirit Himself makes intercession for us with groanings, which cannot be uttered. He who searches the hearts knows what is the mind of the Spirit, because He makes intercession for the saints according to Your will, God.

Romans 8:26-27

PRAYER

The prayer of faith shall save the sick, and You, Lord, shall raise him up.

James 5:15

We are ambassadors for Christ, as though God did beseech you by us, we pray for you in Christ's stead, be reconciled to God. For He has made Him to be sin for us, who knew no sin, that we might be made the righteousness of God in Him.

2 Corinthians 5:20-21

[The apostle Paul said,] "Pray for us, that the word of the Lord may have free course, and be glorified, even as it is with you, and that we may be delivered from unreasonable and wicked men, for not all men have faith. But the Lord is faithful, who shall establish you and keep you from evil."

2 Thessalonians 3:1-3

Prayer can do anything that God can do.

Edward McKendree Bounds

A Christ-like Heart Reflects God's . . .

Respect

"Honor your father and your mother, as the LORD your God has commanded you, that your days may be prolonged, and that it may go well with you."

Deuteronomy 5:16

Bless the LORD, O my soul. O LORD my God, You are very great, You are clothed with honor and majesty.

Psalm 104:1

The one who oppresses the poor reproaches his Maker, but the one who honors Him has mercy on the poor.

Proverbs 14:31

I honor You, LORD, with my substance, and with the first fruits of all my increase, so shall my barns be filled with plenty, and my presses shall burst out with new wine.

Proverbs 3:9

I am as a wonder to many, but You are my strong refuge. Let my mouth be filled with Your praise and with Your honor all the day.

Psalm 71:7-8

Respect

Those members of the body, which I think to be less honorable, upon these I bestow more abundant honor, and our less presentable parts have become much more presentable. For our presentable parts have no need, but You, God, have tempered the body together, having given more abundant honor to that part which lacked.

1 Corinthians 12:23-24

"I, the Father, judge no one, but have committed all judgment to My Son, that all should honor My Son, even as they honor Me, the Father. He who does not honor My Son does not honor Me, the Father, who has sent Him."

John 5:22-23

Let as many servants [employees] under the yoke count their own masters [employers] worthy of all honor, that the name of God and His doctrine be not blasphemed.

1 Timothy 6:1

I shall not be ashamed, when I have respect for all Your commandments.

Psalm 119:6

RESPECT

"Fear Me, your God. Honor the king [government officials]. Servants [employees], be subject to your masters [employers] with all fear, not only to the good and gentle, but also to the perverse. For this is thankworthy, if a person for conscience toward Me endures grief, suffering wrongfully."

1 Peter 2:17-19

"Let the elders who rule well be counted worthy of double honor, especially those who labor in the word and doctrine. For the scripture says, 'You shall not muzzle the ox that treads out the corn.' And, 'The laborer is worthy of his reward.'"

1 Timothy 5:17-18

[The apostle Paul wrote:] "Exhort servants [employees] to be obedient to their own masters [employers], and to please them well in all things, not argumentative, not pilfering, but showing all good fidelity, that they may adorn the doctrine of God our Savior in all things."

Titus 2:9-10

RESPECT

To You, the King eternal, immortal, invisible, the only wise God, be honor and glory forever and ever. Amen.

1 Timothy 1:17

"You younger people, submit yourselves to the elder. Yes, all of you be subject one to another, and be clothed with humility, for I, God, resist the proud, and give grace to the humble."

1 Peter 5:5-6

"Render therefore to all their dues, tax to whom tax is due, revenue to whom revenue, fear to whom fear, honor to whom honor. Owe no one anything, but to love one another, for the one who loves another has fulfilled the law."

Romans 13:7-8

Marriage is honorable in all, and the bed undefiled.

Hebrews 13:4

"Honor widows who are widows indeed. But if any widow has children or grandchildren, let them learn first to show devotion to God at home, and to repay their parents, for that is good and acceptable before Me."

1 Timothy 5:3-4

Respect is what we owe; love is what we give.

Philip James Bailey

A Christ-like Heart Reflects God's . . .

Self-Control

"Better is the end of a thing than the beginning of it, and the patient in spirit is better than the proud in spirit. Be not hasty in your spirit to become angry, for anger rests in the bosom of fools."

Ecclesiastes 7:8-9

"Keep your heart with all diligence, for out of it flow the issues of life."

Proverbs 4:23

"Out of the abundance of the heart the mouth speaks. A good man out of the good treasure of the heart brings forth good things. An evil man brings evil things out of an evil treasure. . . . By your words you shall be justified, and by your words you shall be condemned."

Matthew 12:34-35,37

"You shall be hated by all men for My name's sake, but not a hair of your head will perish. In your patience, possess your souls."

Luke 21:17-19

SELF-CONTROL

Let everyone [even me] be swift to hear, slow to speak, slow to get angry, for human anger does not work the righteousness of God.

James 1:19-20

I, who am slow to get angry, am of great understanding. But the one who is hasty of spirit exalts folly.

Proverbs 14:29

Whoever keeps his mouth and his tongue, keeps his soul from troubles.

Proverbs 21:23

I will take heed to my ways so that I do not sin with my tongue. I will keep my mouth as with a bridle while the wicked is before me.

Psalm 39:1

Even a fool when he keeps his mouth shut, is considered wise. I shut my lips and am esteemed as a person of understanding.

Proverbs 17:28

The fruit of Your Spirit is love, joy, peace, longsuffering, gentleness, goodness, faith, meekness, temperance. There is no law against these things.

Galatians 5:22-23

Self-control

I, who am Christ's, have crucified the flesh with affections and lusts. If I live in the Spirit, let me also walk in the Spirit.

Galatians 5:24-25

If I live after the flesh, I shall die. But if, through the Spirit, I kill the deeds of the body, I shall live.

Romans 8:13

You are a God ready to pardon, gracious and merciful, slow to anger, and very kind. You did not forsake me.

Nehemiah 9:17

Herein is my love made perfect so that I may have boldness in the day of judgment, because as You are, so am I in this world.

1 John 4:17

The one who is void of wisdom despises their neighbor, but a person of understanding holds their peace.

Proverbs 11:12

Self-control is the ability to keep cool while someone is making it hot for you.

Unknown

A CHRIST-LIKE HEART REFLECTS GOD'S . . .

STRENGTH

He said to me, "My grace is sufficient for you, for My strength is made perfect in weakness." Most gladly, then, I will rather glory in my infirmities that the power of Christ may rest upon me . . . for when I am weak, then I am strong.

2 Corinthians 12:9-10

LORD, You are my strength and my shield; my heart trusted in You, and I am helped. Therefore, my heart greatly rejoices and with my song will I praise You. You, LORD, are my strength, and You are the saving strength of Your anointed.

Psalm 28:7-8

You, LORD, are my strength and song, and are become my salvation.

Psalm 118:14

LORD, Your way is strength to the upright, but destruction will come upon the workers of evil.

Proverbs 10:29

STRENGTH

God, You are my strength and power, and You make my way blameless.

2 Samuel 22:33

I know that You save Your anointed [LORD]. You will hear me from Your holy heaven with the saving strength of Your right hand. Some people trust in chariots and some in horses, but I will remember Your name, LORD my God.

Psalm 20:6-7

To You, O my strength, will I sing, for You, God, are my defense and the God of my mercy.

Psalm 59:17

Let the words of my mouth and the meditation of my heart be acceptable in Your sight, O LORD, my strength and my redeemer.

Psalm 19:14

"Be strong in the LORD and in the power of His might. Put on the whole armor of God, so that you may be able to stand against the wiles of the devil."

Ephesians 6:10-11

STRENGTH

Both riches and honor come from You, and You reign over all. In Your hand is power and might; and it is in Your hand to make great and to give strength to all [even me].

1 Chronicles 29:12

The salvation of the righteous is of You, LORD. You are my strength in times of trouble.

Psalm 37:39

"Be strong and of good courage . . . and the LORD—He it is who does go before you. He will be with you. He will not fail you nor forsake you. Fear not, neither be dismayed."

Deuteronomy 31:7-8

You have girded me with strength for battle. You subdued under me those who rose up against me.

2 Samuel 22:40

LORD God, You are my strength, and You will make my feet like deer's feet. You will make me to walk upon my high places.

Habakkuk 3:19

STRENGTH

God, Your weakness is stronger than men.

1 Corinthians 1:25

"Be sober and vigilant, because your adversary the devil walks around like a roaring lion, seeking whom he may devour. Steadfastly resist him in the faith, knowing that the same afflictions are happening to your fellow believers who are in the world."

1 Peter 5:8-9

"Have I not commanded you? Be strong and of good courage. Do not be afraid nor be dismayed, for the LORD your God is with you wherever you go."

Joshua 1:9

LORD, You will give strength to Your people [even me]; You will bless Your people with peace.

Psalm 29:11

"Trust in Me, Your LORD, forever, for in your LORD JEHOVAH is everlasting strength."

Isaiah 26:4

Your eyes, LORD, run to and fro throughout the whole earth, to show Yourself strong in the behalf of those whose heart is perfect toward You.

2 Chronicles 16:9

STRENGTH

LORD, bow down Your ear to me; deliver me speedily; be my strong rock for a house of defense to save me. For You are my rock and my fortress; therefore for Your name's sake lead me and guide me.

Psalm 31:2-3

Glory and honor are in Your presence; strength and gladness are in Your place.

1 Chronicles 16:27

[Israel] did not get the land in possession by their own sword, and neither did their own arm save them, but Your right hand and Your arm and the light of Your countenance, because You favored them. . . . Through You I will push down my enemies; through Your name I will tread over those who rise up against me.

Psalm 44:3,5

When God is our strength, it is strength indeed; when our strength is our own, it is ony weakness.

Augustine of Hippo

A CHRIST-LIKE HEART REFLECTS GOD'S . . .

THANKSGIVING

First of all, I make supplications, prayers, intercessions, and give thanks for all men, for kings and for all that are in authority so that I may lead a quiet and peaceable life in all godliness and honesty.

1 Timothy 2:1-2

Every one of Your creatures is good, and none of them is to be refused, if I receive it with thanksgiving, for it is sanctified by Your word and prayer.

1 Timothy 4:4-5

I give thanks to You, Father, for You have qualified me to partake of the inheritance of the saints in light.

Colossians 1:12

Let me come before Your presence with thanksgiving and make a joyful sound to You with psalms. For You, LORD, are a great God and a great King above all gods.

Psalm 95:2-3

I give thanks to You, LORD, for You are good and Your mercy endures forever.

1 Chronicles 16:34

THANKSGIVING

By Jesus I continually offer the sacrifice of praise to You, God, that is, the fruit of my lips giving thanks to Your name.

Hebrews 13:15

In everything I give You thanks, God, for this is Your will concerning me in Christ Jesus.

1 Thessalonians 5:18

All Your works shall praise You, O LORD, and I shall bless you. I shall speak of the glory of Your kingdom and talk of Your power.

Psalm 145:10-11

For three things I thank God every day of my life: thanks that he has vouchsafed me knowledge of his works; deep thanks that he has set in my darkness the lamp of faith; deep, deepest thanks that I have another life to look forward to— a life joyous with light and flowers and heavenly song.

Helen Adams Keller

A Christ-like Heart Reflects God's . . .

Understanding

God, You make me a person that has understanding of the times, to know what I ought to do.

1 Chronicles 12:32

The fear of You, LORD, is the beginning of wisdom. I have a good understanding because I do Your commandments. Your praise endures forever.

Psalm 111:10

There is no wisdom nor understanding nor counsel that is against You, LORD.

Proverbs 21:30

"My thoughts are not your thoughts, neither are your ways My ways. For as the heavens are higher than the earth, so are My ways higher than your ways and My thoughts than your thoughts."

Isaiah 55:8-9

The one who refuses instruction despises his own soul, but I listen to reprimands and gain understanding.

Proverbs 15:32

God, You are King of all the earth. I sing Your praises with understanding.

Psalm 47:7

UNDERSTANDING

I have more understanding than all my teachers, for Your testimonies are my meditation.

Psalm 119:99

I am a wise-hearted person in whom You, LORD, put wisdom and understanding to know how to do everything You command me to do for Your service.

Exodus 36:1

Counsel in the human heart is like deep water, but a person of understanding [even me] will draw it out.

Proverbs 20:5

Through Your precepts I get understanding, therefore I hate every false way.

Psalm 119:104

The entrance of Your words gives light; it gives understanding to the simple.

Psalm 119:130

How much better is it to get wisdom than gold! And to get understanding is better than to choose silver!

Proverbs 16:16

Understanding

God, I know that Your Son has come and has given me understanding so that I may know Him who is true. I am in Him who is true.

1 John 5:20

Discretion will preserve me, and understanding will keep me. They will deliver me from the way of the evil man.

Proverbs 2:11-12

I forsake the foolish and live. I go in the way of understanding.

Proverbs 9:6

Good understanding gives me favor, but the way of sinners is hard.

Proverbs 13:15

Understanding is a fountain of life to the one who has it, but the instruction of fools is nonsense.

Proverbs 16:22

LORD, give me understanding and I shall keep Your law. Yes, I will observe it with my whole heart.

Psalm 119:34

Understanding

My mouth shall speak of wisdom; and the meditation of my heart shall be of understanding.

Psalm 49:3

The heart of the one who has understanding seeks knowledge, but the mouth of fools feeds on foolishness.

Proverbs 15:14

The one who shuts his lips is esteemed a person of understanding.

Proverbs 17:28

The one who gets wisdom loves his own soul. The one who keeps understanding shall find good.

Proverbs 19:8

Give me, Your servant, an understanding heart . . . that I may discern between good and bad.

1 Kings 3:9

We do not understand
Joy . . . until we face sorrow,
Faith . . . until it is tested,
Peace . . . until faced with conflict,
Trust . . . until we are betrayed,
Love . . . until it is lost,
Hope . . . until confronted with doubts.

Unknown

VISION

Your counsel, LORD, stands forever, the thoughts of Your heart to all generations.

Psalm 33:11

Surely, Lord GOD, You will do nothing, but You reveal Your secret to Your servants the prophets.

Amos 3:7

The LORD answered me, and said, "Write the vision, and make it plain upon tables, that the one may run who reads it. For the vision is yet for an appointed time, but at the end it shall speak, and not lie. Though it tarry, I wait for it, because it will surely come, it will not tarry."

Habakkuk 2:2-3

"Call to Me, and I will answer you, and show you great and mighty things, which you do not know."

Jeremiah 33:3

"'I know the thoughts I think toward you,' says the LORD, 'thoughts of peace, and not of evil, to give you an expected end.'"

Jeremiah 29:11

Vision

God, You reveal the deep and secret things. You know what is in the darkness, and the light dwells with You.

Daniel 2:22

Eye has not seen, nor ear heard, neither has entered into the heart of man, the things which You, God, have prepared for those who love You. But You have revealed them to us by Your Spirit, for the Spirit searches all things, yes, Your deep things, God.

1 Corinthians 2:9-10

"'It shall come to pass in the last days,' says God, 'I will pour out of My Spirit upon all flesh, and your sons and your daughters shall prophesy, and your young men shall see visions, and your old men shall dream dreams. And on My servants and on My handmaidens I will pour out in those days of My Spirit, and they shall prophesy.'"

Acts 2:17-18

A man with the vision of God is not devoted simply to a cause or a particular issue but to God himself.

Oswald Chambers

A Christ-like Heart Reflects God's . . .

Wisdom

The wise in heart will receive commandments, but a chattering fool shall fall.

Proverbs 10:8

I will not be wise in my own eyes. I fear You, LORD, and I depart from evil. This will be health to my body and refreshment to my bones.

Proverbs 3:7-8

Through wisdom is my house built, and by understanding it is established. By knowledge shall the rooms be filled with all precious and pleasant riches.

Proverbs 24:3-4

"I will give you an open mouth and wisdom, which all your adversaries shall not be able to contradict nor resist."

Luke 21:15

In Christ are hidden all the treasures of wisdom and knowledge.

Colossians 2:3

God, You made Christ wisdom, righteousness, sanctification, and redemption to me.

1 Corinthians 1:30

WISDOM

LORD, as Your child, I do not despise Your discipline and I am not weary of Your correction, for You correct those whom You love, LORD, as a father corrects the son he delights in.

Proverbs 3:11-12

Wisdom dwells with good sense, and finds knowledge and discretion.

Proverbs 8:12

The wisdom that You give me is from above. It is first pure, then peaceable, gentle, and easily persuaded, full of mercy and good fruits, impartial, and without hypocrisy.

James 3:17

LORD, You give me wisdom. Out of Your mouth comes knowledge and understanding. You lay up sound wisdom for me who has been made righteous.

Proverbs 2:6-7

Through Your commandments, You have made me wiser than my enemies.

Psalm 119:98

By wisdom my days will be multiplied and the years of my life will be increased.

Proverbs 9:11

I have the mind of Christ.

1 Corinthians 2:16

Wisdom

If I lack wisdom, God, I ask You for it. You give wisdom liberally to me, and You do not reprimand me for asking.

James 1:5

Wisdom is more precious than rubies, and all the things I can desire cannot be compared to her. Long life is in her right hand, and in her left hand are riches and honor. Her ways are pleasant, and all her paths are peaceful. She is a tree of life to me as I lay hold of her, and I am happy because I hold on to her.

Proverbs 3:15-18

The tongue of the wise [even mine] is health.

Proverbs 12:18

You have lavished Your grace on me with all wisdom and good sense.

Ephesians 1:7-8

I will bless You, LORD, who has given me counsel. My innermost being also instructs me in the nighttime.

Psalm 16:7

WISDOM

The words of the wise are heard in quiet more than the cry of the one who rules among fools.

Ecclesiastes 9:17

I have an anointing from the Holy One, and I know the truth.

1 John 2:20

O LORD, how diverse are Your works! In wisdom You have made everything. The earth is full of Your riches.

Psalm 104:24

LORD, by wisdom You have founded the earth; by understanding You have established the heavens.

Proverbs 3:19

I commit my works to You, LORD, and my thoughts will be established.

Proverbs 16:3

Wisdom and knowledge will be the stability of my times and the strength of my salvation.

Isaiah 33:6

Wisdom

Wisdom loves me who loves her; and I seek her early and find her.

Proverbs 8:17

When I hear Jesus' sayings and do them, I am like a wise man who built his house upon a rock.

Matthew 7:24

Your foolishness, God, is wiser than the wisdom of men.

1 Corinthians 1:25

The holy Scriptures are able to make me wise for my salvation through faith which is in Christ Jesus.

2 Timothy 3:15

I am happy when I find wisdom and get understanding, for the profit from it is better than the profit from silver, and what I gain from it is more profitable than the gain from fine gold.

Proverbs 3:13-14

Who knows? God knows and what he knows Is well and best. The darkness hideth not from him, but glows Clear as the morning or the evening rose Of east or west.

Christina Georgina Rossetti

A CHRIST-LIKE HEART REFLECTS GOD'S . . .

ZEAL

The effectual fervent prayer of a righteous person avails much.

James 5:16

Your grace, God, that brings salvation has appeared to all people, teaching us that, denying ungodliness and worldly lusts, we should live soberly, righteously, and godly, in this present world, looking for that blessed hope, and the glorious appearing of the great God and our Savior Jesus Christ, who gave Himself for us, that He might redeem us from all evildoing, and purify to Himself a peculiar people, zealous of good works.

Titus 2:11-14

"Seeing you have purified your souls in obeying the truth through the Spirit to sincere love of the believers, see that you love one another with a pure heart fervently, being born again, not of corruptible seed, but incorruptible, by the word of God, which lives and abides forever."

1 Peter 1:22-23

ZEAL

"Above all things, have fervent love among yourselves, for love shall cover the multitude of sins."

1 Peter 4:8

To us a Child is born, to us a Son is given, and the government shall be upon His shoulder, and His name shall be called Wonderful, Counselor, The mighty God, The everlasting Father, The Prince of Peace. Of the increase of His government and peace there shall be no end. . . . Your zeal, LORD of hosts, will perform this.

Isaiah 9:6-7

"As many as I love, I rebuke and chasten. Be zealous therefore, and repent."

Revelation 3:19

Let a good man do good deeds with the same zeal that the evil man does bad ones.

The Belzer Rabbi

A Teen Relies on God Regarding . . .

God will wither up every spring you have. He will wither up your natural virtues, he will break up confidence in your natural powers, he will wither up your confidence in brain and spirit and body, until you learn by practical experience that you have no right to draw your life from any source other than the tremendous reservoir of the resurrection life of Jesus Christ.

Oswald Chambers

Since we have so great a cloud of witnesses surrounding us, let us also lay aside every encumbrance and the sin which so easily entangles us, and let us run with endurance the race that is set before us.

Hebrews 12:1 NASB

A TEEN RELIES ON GOD REGARDING . . .

ABANDONMENT

Do not cast me off in the time of old age; do not forsake me when my strength fails. For my enemies speak against me, and those who wait for my soul take counsel together, saying, "God has forsaken him; persecute and take him, for there is none to deliver him." O God, be not far from me. O my God, make haste for my help. . . . I will go in Your strength, Lord GOD. I will make mention of Your righteousness, even of Yours only. . . . My tongue also will talk of Your righteousness all the day long, for they are confounded, for they are brought to shame, who seek my hurt.

Psalm 71:9-12,16,24

I have been young, and now am old; yet I have not seen You forsake the righteous, nor his seed begging bread.

Psalm 37:25

ABANDONMENT

LORD, You will not cast off Your people, neither will You forsake Your inheritance.

Psalm 94:14

When I am old and gray, O God, do not forsake me until I have shown Your strength to this generation and Your power to everyone that is to come. Your righteousness also, O God, is very high, who has done great things. O God, who is like You?

Psalm 71:18-19

Do not hide Your face far from me. Do not put me, Your servant, away in anger. You have been my help. Do not leave me, neither forsake me, O God of my salvation. When my father and my mother forsake me, then You, LORD, will take me up.

Psalm 27:9-10

You, LORD, love judgment and do not forsake Your saints. They are preserved forever, but the seed of the wicked will be cut off.

Psalm 37:28

Abandonment

"When the poor and needy seek water and there is none, and their tongue fails for thirst, I the LORD, will hear them; I the God of Israel, will not forsake them. I will open rivers in high places and fountains in the midst of the valleys. I will make the wilderness a pool of water and the dry land springs of water."

Isaiah 41:17-18

Those who know Your name will put their trust in You; for, LORD, You have not forsaken those who seek You.

Psalm 9:10

He has said, "I will never leave you, nor forsake you." So that we may boldly say, "The Lord is my helper, and I will not fear what man shall do to me."

Hebrews 13:5-6

God does not do what false Christianity claims—
keep a person immune from trouble. God says,
"I will be with them in trouble."

Oswald Chambers

Abuse

"After this manner pray: 'Our Father who is in heaven, Hallowed be Your name. Your kingdom come. Your will be done in earth, as it is in heaven. . . . Forgive us our debts, as we forgive our debtors. And do not lead us into temptation, but deliver us from evil.'"

Matthew 6:9-10,12-13

O my God, I trust in You. Do not let me be ashamed; do not let my enemies triumph over me. Yes, do not let any who wait on You be ashamed. Let them be ashamed who transgress without cause. . . . Lead me in Your truth and teach me, for You are the God of my salvation. On You do I wait all day. . . . O keep my soul, and deliver me. Do not let me be ashamed, for I put my trust in You.

Psalm 25:2-3,5,20

Abuse

O LORD my God, in You do I put my trust. Save me from all those who persecute me, and deliver me, lest they tear my soul like a lion, rending it in pieces, while there is none to deliver. . . . Arise, O Lord, in Your anger, lift up Yourself because of the rage of my enemies, and awake for me to the judgment that You have commanded. . . . Oh let the wickedness of the wicked come to an end, but establish the just, for You, the righteous God, try the minds and hearts.

Psalm 7:1-2,6,9

You deliver me from my enemies. Yes, You lift me up above those who rise up against me. You have delivered me from the violent man. Therefore will I give thanks to You, O Lord, among the unbelievers and sing praise to Your name.

Psalm 18:48-49

Abuse

You sent from above, You took me, You drew me out of many waters. You, LORD, delivered me from my strong enemy, and from those who hated me, for they were too strong for me. They confronted me in the day of my calamity, but You, LORD, were my stay. You brought me forth also into a large place. You delivered me, because You delighted in me.

Psalm 18:17-19

You are my hiding place; You will preserve me from trouble; You will surround me with songs of deliverance.

Psalm 32:7

"Whoever shall offend one of the little ones who believes in Me, it would be better for him that a millstone were hanged about his neck, and that he were drowned in the depth of the sea. Woe to the world because of offenses! For it is inevitable that offenses come, but woe to that man by whom the offenses come!"

Matthew 18:6-7

Abuse

In You, O LORD, do I put my trust. Let me never be ashamed; deliver me in Your righteousness. Bow down Your ear to me; deliver me speedily. Be my strong rock, for a house of defense to save me. For You are my rock and my fortress, therefore for Your name's sake lead me and guide me.

Psalm 31:1-3

[Jesus said,] "I do not pray that You should take them out of the world, but that You should keep them from the evil. . . . Sanctify them through Your truth. Your word is truth."

John 17:15,17

Be merciful to me, O God, for man would swallow me up. He, fighting daily, oppresses me. . . . In You, God, have I put my trust. I will not be afraid of what man can do to me. . . . For You have delivered my soul from death. Won't You deliver my feet from falling, that I may walk before You in the light of the living?

Psalm 56:1,11,13

ABUSE

Hear me speedily, O LORD. My spirit fails. Do not hide Your face from me, lest I be like those who go down into the pit. Cause me to hear Your lovingkindess in the morning, for in You do I trust. Cause me to know the way in which I should walk, for I lift up my soul to You. Deliver me, O LORD, from my enemies. I flee to You to hide me. Teach me to do Your will, for You are my God. Your Spirit is good. Lead me into the land of uprightness. Quicken me, O LORD, for Your name's sake. For Your righteousness' sake bring my soul out of trouble. And of Your mercy cut off my enemies, and destroy all those who afflict my soul, for I am Your servant.

Psalm 143:7-12

All cruelty springs from weakness.

Lucius Annaeus Seneca

A Teen Relies on God Regarding . . .

Anger

A wise person fears and departs from evil, but the fool rages and is reckless. The one who is quickly angered deals foolishly. . . . The one who is slow to anger is of great understanding, but the one who is quick-tempered exalts stupidity.

Proverbs 14:16-17,29

"Love your enemies, bless those who curse you, do good to those who hate you, and pray for those who despitefully use you, and persecute you that you may be the children of your Father who is in heaven. For He makes His sun to rise on the evil and on the good, and sends rain on the just and on the unjust."

Matthew 5:44-45

Let everyone be quick to hear, slow to speak, and slow to anger, for human anger does not produce Your righteousness, God.

James 1:19-20

Anger

A soft answer turns away anger. But harsh words stir up anger. . . . A furious person stirs up strife, but the one who is slow to anger calms strife.

Proverbs 15:1,18

"Do all things without grumbling and debating so that you may be blameless and innocent, the sons of God, without rebuke, in the midst of a crooked and perverted nation, among whom you shine as a light in the world."

Philippians 2:14-15

The discretion of a person defers their anger, and it is to their glory to pass over a transgression.

Proverbs 19:11

The one who is slow to anger is better than the mighty; and the one who rules their spirit than the one who captures a city.

Proverbs 16:32

The one who despises their neighbor sins; but the one who has mercy on the poor [this one] is happy.

Proverbs 14:21

A wise person turns away wrath.

Proverbs 29:8

Anger

"Put away lying; speak truth with your neighbor, for we are members of one another. Be angry but do not sin. Do not let the sun go down on your wrath."

Ephesians 4:25-26

"All the law is fulfilled in one word, even in this: You shall love your neighbor as yourself. But if you bite and devour one another, take heed that you do not consume one another. This I say then, 'Walk in the Spirit, and you will not fulfill the lust of the flesh.'"

Galatians 5:14-16

"Put off all these: anger, wrath, malice . . . seeing that you have put off the old person with their deeds and have put on the new person, which is renewed in knowledge after the image of Me who created you."

Colossians 3:8,10

God hugs you.

Hildegarde of Bingen

A Teen Relies on God Regarding . . .

Anxiety

Cause me to hear Your lovingkindness in the morning, for in You do I trust. Cause me to know the way in which I should walk; for I lift up my soul to You. . . . Teach me to do Your will, for You are my God. Your Spirit is good. Lead me into the land of uprightness. . . . For Your righteousness' sake bring my soul out of trouble.

Psalm 143:8,10-11

It is vain for me to rise up early, to sit up late, to eat the bread of sorrows, for You give Your beloved sleep.

Psalm 127:2

I have trusted also in You, LORD; therefore I shall not slide.

Psalm 26:1

"Humble yourself . . . casting all your care upon Me, for I care for you."

1 Peter 5:6-7

When I said, "My foot slips," Your mercy, O LORD, held me up.

Psalm 94:18

Anxiety

Surely I shall not be moved forever. The righteous shall be in everlasting remembrance. I shall not be afraid of evil tidings. My heart is fixed, trusting in You, LORD.

Psalm 112:6-7

Show Your marvelous lovingkindness, O You who save by Your right hand those who put their trust in You from those who rise up against them. Keep me as the apple of the eye; hide me under the shadow of Your wings.

Psalm 17:7-8

I have set you, LORD, always before me; because You are at my right hand, I shall not be moved. Therefore my heart is glad, and my glory rejoices. My flesh also shall rest in hope.

Psalm 16:8-9

I will both lay myself down in peace, and sleep, for You only, LORD, make me dwell in safety.

Psalm 4:7

Anxiety has its use, stimulating us to seek
with keener longing for that security
where peace is complete and unassailable.

Augustine of Hippo

A Teen Relies on God Regarding . . .

Attitude

"Let this mind be in you, which was also in Christ Jesus, who, being in the form of God, thought it not robbery to be equal with God, but made Himself of no reputation, and took upon Himself the form of a servant, and was made in the likeness of men. And being found in fashion as a man, He humbled Himself, and became obedient to death, even the death of the cross. For this I, God, also have highly exalted Him, and given Him a name which is above every name."

Philippians 2:5-9

"You shall love the Lord your God with all your heart, and with all your soul, and with all your strength, and with all your mind, and your neighbor as yourself. . . . Do this and you shall live."

Luke 10:27-28

ATTITUDE

"Be renewed in the spirit of your mind, and put on the new man, which after God is created in righteousness and true holiness."

Ephesians 4:23-24

"Put on therefore, as the chosen of God, holy and beloved, a merciful heart, kindness, humility, meekness, longsuffering, forbearing one another, and forgiving one another, if anyone has a quarrel against any, even as Christ forgave you, so also do you. And above all these things put on love, which is the perfect bond of unity."

Colossians 3:12-14

"Do all things without murmurings and disputings, that you may be blameless and harmless, the sons of God, without rebuke, in the midst of a crooked and perverse nation, among whom you shine as lights in the world."

Philippians 2:14-15

Who has known the mind of the Lord, so as to instruct Him? But I have the mind of Christ.

1 Corinthians 2:16

Attitude

"Gird up the loins of your mind, be sober, and hope to the end for the grace that is to be brought to you at the revelation of Jesus Christ, as obedient children, not fashioning yourselves according to the former lusts in your ignorance. But as He who has called you is holy, so you be holy in all manner of life, because it is written, 'Be holy, for I am holy.'"

1 Peter 1:13-16

All of you be of one mind, having compassion one for another, love one another, be sympathetic, be courteous, not repaying evil for evil, or abuse for abuse, but on the contrary, blessing, knowing that you are called to this, that you should inherit a blessing.

1 Peter 3:8-9

[Moses said,] "I have set before you life and death, blessing and cursing, therefore choose life, that both you and your seed may live."

Deuteronomy 30:19

Attitude

"Serve Me your LORD, with gladness. Come before My presence with singing. Know that I, the LORD, AM God. It is I who has made you, and not you yourselves. You are My people, and the sheep of My pasture. Enter into My gates with thanksgiving, and into My courts with praise. Be thankful to Me, and bless My name. For I am good; My mercy is everlasting, and My truth endures to all generations."

Psalm 100:2-5

"And I will give you one heart, and I will put a new spirit within you. And I will take the stony heart out of your flesh and will give you a heart of flesh that you may walk in my statutes and keep my ordinances, and do them. And you shall be my people, and I will be your God."

Ezekiel 11:19-20

The greater part of our happiness depends on our disposition and not our circumstances.

Martha Washington

A Teen Relies on God Regarding . . .

Conflict

"You do not wrestle against flesh and blood, but against principalities, against powers, against the rulers of the darkness of this world, against spiritual wickedness in high places. Wherefore take the whole armor of God, that you may be able to withstand in the evil day."

Ephesians 6:12

Christ also suffered for me, leaving me an example, that I should follow His steps. . . . When He was insulted, He did not insult in reply. When He suffered, He did not threaten but committed Himself to You who judges righteously.

1 Peter 2:21,23

You shall hide me in the secret of Your presence from the snares of man. You shall keep me secretly in a pavilion from the strife of tongues.

Psalm 31:20

Cast out the scoffer and contention will go out; yes, strife and shame shall cease.

Proverbs 22:10

Conflict

Many are the afflictions of the righteous, but You, LORD, deliver them out of them all.

Psalm 34:19

Where no wood is, the fire goes out. Similarly, where there is no talebearer, the strife ceases.

Proverbs 26:20

The one who is of a proud heart, stirs up strife; but the one who puts his trust in You, LORD, shall be satisfied.

Proverbs 28:25

"When you stand praying, forgive, if you have anything against anyone so that Your Father who is in heaven may forgive you your offenses. But if you do not forgive, neither will your Father forgive you for your offenses."

Mark 11:25-26

"Be complete, be of good comfort, be of one mind, live in peace; and, I, the God of love and peace will be with you."

2 Corinthians 13:11

When a person's ways please You, LORD, You make even their enemies to be at peace with them.

Proverbs 16:7

Conflict

It is an honor for me to cease from strife, but every fool will be meddling.

Proverbs 20:3

I, who love my brother, dwell in the light; and there is no occasion of stumbling in me. But the one who hates his brother is in darkness and walks in darkness and doesn't know where he is going, because that darkness has blinded his eyes.

1 John 2:10-11

"Pursue peace with all people, and holiness, without which you shall not see Me, your Lord."

Hebrews 12:14

I will cry to You, God most high, to You who performs all things for me. You shall send from heaven and save me from the reproach of the one who would swallow me up. You shall send forth Your mercy and Your truth.

Psalm 57:2-3

Would not the carrying out of one single commandment of Christ, "Love one another," change the whole aspect of the world and sweep away prisons and workhouses, and envying and strife, and all the strongholds of the devil?

Max Muller

A Teen Relies on God Regarding . . .

Confusion

God, You are not the author of confusion, but of peace.

1 Corinthians 14:33

"Let the peace of God rule in your hearts, to which also you are called in one body, and be thankful."

Colossians 3:15

Where envying and strife is, there is confusion and every evil work. But the wisdom that is from above is first pure, then peaceable, gentle, and easy to be entreated, full of mercy and good fruits, without partiality, and without hypocrisy.

James 3:16-17

"You, My sheep, hear My voice, and I call you, My own sheep, by name, and lead you out. And when I put forth My own sheep, I go before you, and you, My sheep, follow Me, for you know My voice. And a stranger you will not follow, but will flee from him, for you do not know the voice of strangers."

John 10:3-5

Confusion

"Everyone who is of the truth hears My voice."

John 18:37

Your word is a lamp to my feet, and a light to my path.

Psalm 119:105

Cause me to hear Your lovingkindess in the morning; for in You do I trust. Cause me to know the way in which I should walk, for I lift up my soul to You.

Psalm 143:8

Lead me, O LORD, in Your righteousness because of my enemies. Make Your way straight before my face.

Psalm 5:8

In You, O LORD, do I put my trust. Never let me be put to confusion. Deliver me in Your righteousness, and cause me to escape. Incline Your ear to me, and save me. Be my strong habitation, where I may continually resort. You have given commandment to save me, for You are my rock and my fortress.

Psalm 71:1-3

CONFUSION

"I will bring the blind by a way that they did not know, I will lead them in paths that they have not known. I will make darkness light before them, and crooked things straight. These things will I do to them, and not forsake them."

Isaiah 42:16

"If any of you lack wisdom, ask of Me, who gives to all liberally and does not reprimand you for asking, and it shall be given to you. But ask in faith, with no wavering. For the one who wavers is like a wave of the sea driven with the wind and tossed. . . . A double minded person is unstable in all ways."

James 1:5-6,8

"Be still, and know that I am God. I will be exalted among the unbelieving nations. I will be exalted in the earth."

Psalm 46:10-11

The greatest moments of your life are those when through all the confusion God got a message through to you plain and certain.

Bertha Munro

A TEEN RELIES ON GOD REGARDING . . .

DEPRESSION

The sorrows of death surround me. . . . The sorrows of hell surround me on every side; the noose of death goes before me. In my distress I called upon You, LORD, and cried to You, my God. You heard my voice out of Your temple, and my cry came before You into Your ears. . . . You sent from above, You took me and drew me out of many waters.

Psalm 18:4-6,16

You, LORD, preserve the simple. I was brought low, and You helped me. Return to your rest, O my soul; for the LORD, has dealt bountifully with you. For You [LORD] have delivered my soul from death, my eyes from tears, and my feet from falling.

Psalm 116:6-8

LORD, You will be a refuge for the oppressed, a refuge in times of trouble.

Psalm 9:9

Depression

You deliver me in my affliction when I am poor and open my ears in oppressions.

Job 36:15

How long shall I take counsel in my soul, having sorrow in my heart daily? . . .Consider and hear me, O LORD my God. Lighten my eyes, lest I sleep the sleep of death. . . . But I have trusted in Your mercy; my heart shall rejoice in Your salvation.

Psalm 13:2-3,5

LORD, You will give me rest from my sorrow, and from my fear, and from the hard bondage in which I was made to serve.

Isaiah 14:3

You satisfy my longing soul and fill my hungry soul with goodness.

Psalm 107:9

God, You anointed Jesus of Nazareth with the Holy Spirit and with power, who went about doing good and healing all who were oppressed of the devil, for You were with Him.

Acts 10:38

DEPRESSION

I will be glad and rejoice in Your mercy, for You have considered my trouble; You have known my soul in adversities.

Psalm 31:7

You will fulfill the desire of those who fear You. You also will hear their cry and will save them. You, LORD, preserve all who love You.

Psalm 145:19-20

O LORD, You have brought up my soul from the grave. You have kept me alive that I should not go down to the pit.

Psalm 30:3

Your anger endures but a moment; in Your favor is life. Weeping may endure for a night, but joy comes in the morning.

Psalm 30:5

LORD, You execute judgment for me when I am oppressed. You give food to me when I am hungry. LORD, You loose me when I am prisoner. You open my eyes when they are blind. You raise me when I am bowed down. You love the righteous [even me].

Psalm 146:7-8

Depression

My heart is sore pained within me, and the terrors of death are fallen upon me. Fearfulness and trembling are come upon me, and horror has overwhelmed me. . . . As for me, I will call upon You, God, and You shall save me. Evening, and morning and at noon will I pray and cry aloud; and You shall hear my voice.

Psalm 55:4-5,16-17

Do not let the flood overflow me, neither let the deep swallow me up, and do not let the pit shut her mouth upon me. Hear me, O LORD, for Your lovingkindness is good. Turn to me according to the multitude of Your tender mercies. And hide not Your face from Your servant, for I am in trouble. Hear me speedily.

Psalm 69:15-17

When I cried to You, the LORD God of my fathers, You heard my voice and looked on my affliction, and my labor, and my oppression.

Deuteronomy 26:7

Depression

O God, You are my God; I will seek You early. My soul thirsts for You, my flesh longs for You in a dry and thirsty land, where no water is. . . . Because You have been my help, therefore in the shadow of Your wings I will rejoice.

Psalm 63:1,7-8

As the deer pants after the water brooks, so pants my soul after You, O God. My soul thirsts for You, for the living God. When shall I come and appear before You? My tears have been my meat day and night, while they continually say to me, "Where is your God?" . . . Deep calls to deep at the noise of your waterspouts. All Your waves and Your billows are gone over me. Yet You, LORD, will command Your lovingkindness in the daytime, and in the night Your song shall be with me, and my prayer to You, the God of my life.

Psalm 42:1-4,7-8

DEPRESSION

My offenses have gone over my head, as a heavy burden, they are too heavy for me. . . . I am troubled; I am bowed down greatly; I go mourning all the day long. . . . My heart pants, my strength fails me. As for the light of my eyes, it also is gone from me. . . . In You, O LORD, do I hope. You will hear, O Lord my God. . . . Do not forsake me, LORD. O my God, do not be far from me. Make haste to help me, O Lord of my salvation.

Psalm 38:4,6,10,15,21-22

The dayspring from on high has visited me, to give me light, who sits in darkness and in the shadow of death, to guide my feet into the way of peace.

Luke 1:78-79

The best cure for an empty day or a longing heart is to find people who need you. Look, the world is full of them.

Unknown

A Teen Relies on God Regarding . . .

Discipline

The fruit of the Spirit is . . . self-control.

Galatians 5:22-23

Everyone who strives for the mastery is temperate in all things. Now they do it to obtain a corruptible crown, but we an incorruptible. . . . I keep my body under, and bring it into subjection, lest that by any means, when I have preached to others, I myself should be a castaway.

1 Corinthians 9:25,27

"Giving all diligence, add to your faith virtue, and to virtue knowledge, and to knowledge temperance, and to temperance patience, and to patience godliness, and to godliness brotherly kindness, and to brotherly kindness love. For if these things are in you, and abound, they make you that you shall neither be barren nor unfruitful in the knowledge of our Lord Jesus Christ."

2 Peter 1:5-8

Discipline

Bodily exercise profits little, but godliness is profitable in all things, having promise of the life that now is, and of that which is to come.

1 Timothy 4:8

The soul of the sluggard desires, and has nothing, but the soul of the diligent shall be satisfied.

Proverbs 13:4

See the one diligent in business? They shall stand before kings; they shall not stand before insignificant people.

Proverbs 22:29

The hand of the diligent shall rule, but the slothful shall be under forced labor.

Proverbs 12:24

"This book of the law shall not depart out of your mouth; but you shall meditate in it day and night, that you may observe to do according to all that is written in it, for then you will make your way prosperous, and then you will have good success."

Joshua 1:8

Do not consider painful what is good for you.

Euripides

Discouragement

You lead me beside still waters. You restore my soul.

Psalm 23:2-3

"Repent and be converted, that your sins may be blotted out, when the times of refreshing shall come from the presence of your Lord."

Acts 3:19

Let me not be weary in well doing, for in due season I shall reap, if I faint not.

Galatians 6:9

If I give out my soul to the hungry and satisfy the afflicted soul, then will my light rise in obscurity and my darkness will be as the noonday. You, LORD, will guide me continually and satisfy my soul in drought and strengthen my bones. I shall be like a watered garden and like a spring of water, whose waters do not fail.

Isaiah 58:10-11

You keep track of my wanderings. You put my tears into Your bottle. Are they not in Your book?

Psalm 56:8

Discouragement

My soul is melted because of trouble. . . . I am at my wit's end. Then I cry out to You, LORD, in my trouble, and You bring me out of my distresses. You make the storm calm so that the waves are still. Then I am glad because they are quiet, and You bring me to my desired haven.

Psalm 107:26-30

My flesh and my heart fail, but You, God, are the strength of my heart and my portion forever.

Psalm 73:26

You, LORD, are good to all, and Your tender mercies are over all Your works.

Psalm 145:9

Because I have set my love upon You, You will deliver me. You will set me on high, because I have known Your name. I will call on You, and You will answer me. You will be with me in trouble; You will deliver me and honor me.

Psalm 91:14-15

Discouragement

The hope of the righteous shall be gladness, but the expectation of the wicked will perish.

Proverbs 10:28

Strangers have risen up against me, and oppressors seek after my soul. They have not set You, God, before them. Behold, You, God, are my help. You are with those who uphold my soul.

Psalm 54:3-4

I will remember the years of Your right hand, most High. I will remember Your works, LORD. Surely I will remember Your wonders of old. I will meditate also on all Your work and talk of Your doings. Your way, O God, is in the sanctuary. Who is so great a God as our God? You are the God who does wonders. You have declared Your strength among the people

Psalm 77:10-14

[I am] strengthened with all might, according to Your glorious power, to all patience and longsuffering with joyfulness.

Colossians 1:11

Discouragement

Hear me when I call, O God of my righteousness. You have enlarged me when I was in distress. Have mercy on me, and hear my prayer.

Psalm 4:1

Happy am I who have You, the God of Jacob for my help, whose hope is in You, LORD.

Psalm 146:5

Great are Your tender mercies, O LORD. Revive me according to Your judgments.

Psalm 119:156

Whom do I have in heaven but You? There is none on the earth whom I desire beside You. . . . It is good for me to draw near to You, God. I have put my trust in You so that I may declare all Your works.

Psalm 73:25,28

"Not one sparrow will fall on the ground without your Father. But the very hairs on your head are all numbered; therefore, do not fear. You are of more value than many sparrows."

Matthew 10:29-30

Discouragement

I laid myself down and slept. I awoke, for LORD, You sustained me.

Psalm 3:5

Hope deferred makes my heart sick, but when my desire comes, it is a tree of life.

Proverbs 13:12

Delight yourself also in Me, your LORD, and I will give you the desires of your heart.

Psalm 37:4

You have not despised nor abhorred the affliction of the afflicted; neither have You hidden Your face from me; but when I cried to You, You heard. My praise shall be of You in the great congregation.

Psalm 22:24-25

Who shall ascend into Your holy hill, LORD? Or who shall stand in Your holy place? The one who has clean hands and a pure heart, who has not lifted up their soul to vanity, nor sworn deceitfully. He shall receive the blessing from You, LORD, and righteousness from You, the God of his salvation.

Psalm 24:3-5

When we yield to discouragement, it is usually because we give too much thought to the past or to the future.

Therese of Lisieux

A Teen Relies on God Regarding . . .

Doubt

Faith comes by hearing, and hearing by Your word, God.

Romans 10:17

This is the confidence that I have in You, that, if I ask anything according to Your will, You hear me, and if I know that You hear me, whatever I ask, I know that I have the petitions that I desire of You.

1 John 5:14

If you shall say to this mountain, "Be removed, and be cast into the sea," and shall not doubt in your heart, but shall believe that those things which you say shall come to pass, you shall have whatever you say.

Mark 11:23

Jesus said to him, "If you can believe, all things are possible to you who believe." And right away the father of the child cried out, and said with tears, "Lord, I believe; help my unbelief."

Mark 9:24-25

DOUBT

"Believe in the LORD your God, so shall you be established; believe His prophets, so shall you prosper."

2 Chronicles 20:20

"These things I have written to you who believe on the name of the Son of God; that you may know that you have eternal life, and that you may believe on the name of the Son of God."

1 John 5:13

These [things] are written, that I might believe that Jesus is the Christ, Your Son, God; and that believing I might have life through His name.

John 20:31

"Ask in faith, nothing wavering. For the one who wavers is like a wave of the sea driven with the wind and tossed. For the doubter should not expect to receive anything of the Lord. A double-minded person is unstable in all ways."

James 1:6-8

Every step toward Christ kills a doubt.
Every thought, word, and deed for him
carries you away from discouragement.

Theodore Ledyard Cuyler

A TEEN RELIES ON GOD REGARDING . . .

FAILURE

Who is the one who condemns? It is Christ who died, yes, rather who is risen again. He is even at Your right hand, God, making intercession for me.

Romans 8:34

"Return to me, the LORD your God. . . . I will heal your backsliding, I will love you freely, for My anger is turned away from you."

Hosea 14:1,4

Don't rejoice against me, O my enemy, for when I fall, I shall arise; when I sit in darkness, the LORD, shall be a light to me.

Micah 7:8

LORD, You uphold all who fall and raise up all who are bowed down [even me].

Psalm 145:14

Thanks be to You, God, who always causes me to triumph in Christ.

2 Corinthians 2:14

A just person falls seven times, and rises up again.

Proverbs 24:16

Failure

"When you pass through the waters, I will be with you; and through the rivers, they will not overflow you. When you walk through the fire, you shall not be burned nor will the flame consume you. For I am the LORD your God, the Holy One of Israel, your Savior."

Isaiah 43:2-3

Lord, You are good and ready to forgive. You are abundant in mercy to all who call on You [even me].

Psalm 86:5

LORD, You are gracious and full of compassion; slow to get angry and of great mercy.

Psalm 145:8

The one who covers his sins will not prosper, but whoever confesses and forsakes them, will have mercy.

Proverbs 28:13

Who is a God like You, who pardons evildoing and passes by the transgression of the remnant of His heritage? You do not retain your anger forever because You delight in mercy.

Micah 7:18-19

FAILURE

"Return, you backsliding child, and I will heal your backslidings. Behold, I come to you; for you are the LORD my God."

Jeremiah 3:22

All have sinned and come short of Your glory, God. You have justified me freely by Your grace through the redemption that is in Christ Jesus.

Romans 3:23-24

"Humble yourself under My mighty hand, so that I may exalt you in due time."

1 Peter 5:6

Like a father has compassion on his children, so You, LORD, have compassion on me, who fears You. For You know my frame; You remember that I am dust.

Psalm 103:13-14

If I confess my sins, You are faithful and just to forgive me my sins and to cleanse me from all unrighteousness.

1 John 1:9

Bless the LORD, O my soul. . . . [He] redeems my life from destruction; [He] crowns me with lovingkindness and tender mercies.

Psalm 103:1,4

FAILURE

All things work together for good to those [like me] who love You and who are called according to Your purpose.

Romans 8:28

You will have compassion on me according to the multitude of Your mercies.

Lamentations 3:32

You have made me a little lower than the angels and have crowned me with glory and honor. You made me to have dominion over the works of Your hands. You have put all things under my feet.

Psalm 8:5-6

You, LORD, will bless the righteous; with favor you will surround me as with a shield.

Psalm 5:12

LORD, how are they increased who trouble me! Many are they who rise up against me. Many are there who say of my soul, "There is no help for him in God." But You, O LORD, are a shield for me, my glory and the lifter up of my head. I cried to You, LORD, with my voice, and You heard me out of Your holy hill.

Psalm 3:1-4

Failure

I am confident of this very thing, that You who has begun a good work in me will perform it until the day of Jesus Christ.

Philippians 1:6

Who shall separate me from the love of Christ? Shall tribulation, or distress, or persecution, or famine, or nakedness, or peril, or sword? . . . No, in all these things, I am more than a conqueror through [Christ] who loved me.

Romans 8:35,37

Though I fall, I shall not be utterly cast down; for You, LORD, uphold me with Your hand.

Psalm 37:24

LORD, You take pleasure in those [like me] who fear You and in those [like me] who hope in Your mercy.

Psalm 147:11

Success consists of getting up more times than you fall.

Oliver Goldsmith

Fear

A thousand shall fall at my side and ten thousand at my right hand, but it will not come near me. Only with my eyes shall I behold and see the reward of the wicked. Because I have made You, LORD, who are my refuge, even You, the most High, my habitation, no evil will befall me, neither will any plague come near my dwelling.

Psalm 91:7-10

I will be secure, because there is hope . . . I will take my rest in safety. Also I will lie down and none will make me afraid.

Job 11:18-19

You are my hiding place and my shield. I hope in Your word. . . . Hold me up, and I shall be safe. And I will have respect for Your laws continually.

Psalm 119:114,117

FEAR

"Be of good courage and I shall strengthen your heart, all you who hope in the LORD."

Psalm 31:24

It is vain for me to rise up early, to sit up late, and eat the bread of sorrows, for You give Your beloved sleep.

Psalm 127:2

There is no fear in love, but perfect love casts out fear, because fear has torment.

1 John 4:18

"Thus says the LORD who created you, . . . 'Fear not, for I have redeemed you. I have called you by your name; you are Mine.'"

Isaiah 43:1

"Cast your burden upon Me, your LORD, and I will sustain you. I will never allow the righteous to be moved."

Psalm 55:22

"Peace I leave with you, My peace I give to you, not as the world gives do I give to you. Do not let your heart be troubled, neither let it be afraid."

John 14:27

FEAR

I sought You, LORD, and You heard me, and delivered me from all my fears.

Psalm 34:4

No weapon that is formed against me will prosper, and every tongue that will rise against me in judgment You will condemn. This is the heritage of Your servants, LORD, and my righteousness is of You.

Isaiah 54:17

"Fear not, for I am with you. Do not be dismayed, for I am your God. I will strengthen you; yes, I will help you; yes, I will uphold you with the right hand of My righteousness."

Isaiah 41:10

"Whoever hearkens to Me will dwell safely and will be quiet from fear of evil."

Proverbs 1:33

I have not received the spirit of bondage again to fear, but I have received the Spirit of adoption, by whom I cry, "Abba, Father."

Romans 8:15

Fear

Though I walk through the valley of the shadow of death, I will fear no evil, for You are with me. Your rod and Your staff comfort me.

Psalm 23:4

The LORD is my light and my salvation; whom shall I fear? The LORD is the strength of my life; of whom shall I be afraid? . . . Though an army should encamp against me, my heart will not fear. Though war rises against me, in this I will be confident.

Psalm 27:1,3

You are the LORD; You do not change.

Malachi 3:6

"'For the oppression of the poor, for the sighing of the needy, now will I arise,' says the LORD; 'I will set you in safety from the one who threatens you.'"

Psalm 12:5

No coward soul is mine, No trembler in the world's storm-troubled sphere; I see Heaven's glories shine, And faith shine equal, arming me from fear.

Emily Brontë

A TEEN RELIES ON GOD REGARDING . . .

FRUSTRATION

LORD, You are my strength and my shield; my heart trusts in You, and I am helped. Therefore my heart greatly rejoices, and with my song will I praise You.

Psalm 28:7

"Do not fret because of evil people, neither be envious at the wicked, for there shall be no reward to the evil person; the candle of the wicked shall be put out."

Proverbs 24:19

"Commit your way to the LORD; trust also in Him, and He shall bring it to pass. . . . Rest in the LORD, and wait patiently for Him. Do not fret because of the one who prospers in his way, because of the one who brings wicked devices to pass."

Psalm 37:5,7

I taste and see that You, LORD, are good. Blessed are those who trust in You.

Psalm 34:8

Frustration

As for You, God, Your way is perfect. Your word, LORD, is tried.

Psalm 18:30

It is better to trust in You, LORD, than to put confidence in people.

Psalm 118:8

"Trust in Me, your LORD with all your heart, and do not lean on your own understanding. In all your ways acknowledge Me, and I shall direct your paths."

Proverbs 3:5-6

Deliver me in Your righteousness, LORD, and cause me to escape. Incline Your ear to me, and save me. Be my strong habitation, where I may continually resort. You have given commandment to save me, for You are my rock and my fortress.

Psalm 71:2

My times are in Your hand, Lord. Deliver me from the hand of my enemies, and from those who persecute me.

Psalm 31:15

He didn't say, You will not be tossed around,
You will not have hard trials, You will not be afflicted;
But he said, You will not be overcome.

Julian of Norwich (Modernized)

A Teen Relies on God Regarding . . .

Gossip

"Keep your heart with all diligence, for out of it are the issues of life. Put away from yourself a perverse mouth, and perverse lips put far from yourself."

Proverbs 4:23-24

It is Your glory, God, to conceal a thing.

Proverbs 25:2

The one who hides hatred with lying lips, and the one who utters a slander, is a fool . . . but the one who refrains his lips is wise.

Proverbs 10:18-19

Let the lying lips be put to silence that speak grievous things proudly and contemptuously against the righteous. Oh how great is Your goodness, which You have laid up for those who fear You; which you have wrought for those who trust in You before the sons of men! You shall hide them in the secret of your presence from human pride. You shall keep them secretly in a pavilion from the strife of tongues.

Psalm 31:18-19

GOSSIP

The one who goes about as a talebearer reveals secrets, therefore I do not meddle with the one who flatters with his lips.

Proverbs 20:19

LORD, You shall cut off all flattering lips, and the tongue that speaks proud things.

Psalm 12:3

"Hear, for I [Wisdom] will speak of excellent things, and the opening of my lips shall reveal right things. . . . All the words of my mouth are in righteousness."

Proverbs 8:6,8

Who is the one that desires life and loves many days, that he may see good? Keep your tongue from evil and your lips from speaking guile.

Psalm 34:12-13

In my distress I cried to the LORD, and He heard me. Deliver my soul, O LORD, from lying lips, and from a deceitful tongue.

Psalm 120:1-2

Where no wood is, there the fire goes out; so where there is no talebearer, the strife ceases..

Proverbs 26:20

Gossip

The lips of the righteous know what is acceptable, but the mouth of the wicked speaks perverseness.

Proverbs 10:32

The one who keeps his mouth keeps his life, but the one who opens wide his lips shall have destruction.

Proverbs 13:3

"Go from the presence of a foolish person, when you do not perceive in him the lips of knowledge. The wisdom of the prudent is to understand his way, but the folly of fools is deceit."

Proverbs 14:7-8

A fool's lips enter into contention. . . . A fool's mouth is his destruction, and his lips are the snare of his soul. The words of a talebearer are as wounds, and they go down into the innermost parts of the belly.

Proverbs 18:6-8

The wicked is snared by the transgression of his lips, but the just shall come out of trouble.

Proverbs 12:13

Gossip

Righteous lips are the delight of kings, and they love him who speaks right.

Proverbs 16:13

Death and life are in the power of the tongue, and those who love it shall eat the fruit of it.

Proverbs 18:21

The one who handles a matter wisely shall find good; and whoever trusts in the Lord, happy are they. The wise in heart shall be called prudent; and the sweetness of the lips increases learning.

Proverbs 16:20-21

The one who will love life and see good days, let him refrain his tongue from evil and his lips from speaking guile.

1 Peter 3:10

LORD, who shall abide in Your tabernacle? . . . The one who does not backbite with his tongue, nor does evil to his neighbor, nor takes up a reproach against his neighbor.

Psalm 15:1,3

A gossip usually makes a mountain out of a molehill by adding some dirt.

Unknown

A Teen Relies on God Regarding . . .

Greed

Paul wrote, "Having food and clothes let us be content. But those who will be rich fall into temptation and a snare, and into many foolish and hurtful lusts, which drown people in destruction and ruin. For the love of money is the root of all evil, which while some coveted after, they have erred from the faith, and pierced themselves through with many sorrows. But you, O man of God, flee these things, and follow after righteousness."

1 Timothy 6:8-11

[The slothful] covets greedily all day long, but the righteous give and spare not.

Proverbs 21:26

Those who are greedy of gain trouble their own houses, but those who hate bribes shall live.

Proverbs 15:27

Hell and destruction are never full so the eyes of people are never satisfied.

Proverbs 27:20

Greed

Let your character be without covetousness and be content with such things as you have, for He has said, "I will ever leave you, nor forsake you."

Hebrews 13:5

Godliness with contentment is great gain. For I brought nothing into this world, and it is certain I can carry nothing out.

1 Timothy 6:6-7

The cares of this world, and deceitfulness of riches, and the lusts of other things entering in, choke the word, and it becomes unfruitful. And these are they which are sown on good ground, such as hear the word, and receive it, and bring forth fruit.

Mark 4:19-20

I do not speak in respect of want, for I have learned, in whatever state I am, to be content. I know how to be abased, and I know how to abound. . . . I can do all things through Christ who strengthens me.

Philippians 4:11-13

The ones who seek more than they need hinder themselves from enjoying what they have.

Hebrew Proverb

A TEEN RELIES ON GOD REGARDING . . .

GRIEF

"The Spirit of the Lord GOD is upon me because the LORD has anointed me to preach good tidings to the meek. He has sent me to bind up the brokenhearted, to proclaim liberty to the captives, and the opening of the prison to those who are bound; to proclaim the acceptable year of the LORD, and the day of vengeance of our God; to comfort all who mourn; to appoint to those who mourn in Zion, to give to them beauty for ashes, the oil of joy for mourning, the garment of praise for the spirit of heaviness; that they might be called trees of righteousness, the planting of the LORD, that He might be glorified."

Isaiah 61:1-3

He is despised and rejected of men, a man of sorrow and acquainted with grief. . . . Surely He has borne my griefs and carried my sorrows.

Isaiah 53:3-4

Grief

You will not break a bruised reed, and the smoking wick, You will not quench. You will bring forth justice.

Isaiah 42:3

You heal the broken in heart and bind up their wounds.

Psalm 147:3

Your ransomed ones, LORD, shall return and come to Zion with songs and everlasting joy upon their heads. They shall obtain joy and gladness, and sorrow and sighing will flee away.

Isaiah 35:10

My eye is consumed because of grief; it grows old because of all my enemies. Depart from me, all you workers of evil, for the LORD has heard the voice of my weeping. The LORD has heard my supplication; the LORD will receive my prayer.

Psalm 6:7-9

It is of Your mercies, LORD, that we are not consumed, because Your compassions do not fail. They are new every morning. Great is Your faithfulness.

Lamentations 3:22-23

Grief

"The redeemed of the LORD shall return and come with singing to Zion, and everlasting joy will be upon their heads. They shall obtain gladness and joy, and sorrow and mourning shall flee away. I, even I, am He who comforts you."

Isaiah 51:11-12

"Blessed are you who mourn, for you will be comforted."

Matthew 5:4

Now our Lord Jesus Christ Himself and You, my Father, have loved us and have given us everlasting consolation and good hope through grace. Comfort our hearts and establish us in every good word and work.

2 Thessalonians 2:16-17

You, LORD, will comfort Zion. You will comfort all her waste places, and You will make her wilderness like Eden and her desert like Your garden, LORD. Joy and gladness will be found there, thanksgiving and the voice of melody.

Isaiah 51:3

I who sow in tears will reap in joy.

Psalm 126:5

Grief

Hear, O LORD, and have mercy on me. LORD, be my helper. You have turned my mourning into dancing. You have put off my sackcloth and surrounded me with gladness.

Psalm 30:10-11

LORD, You have comforted Your people and will have mercy on Your afflicted. . . . "I have engraved you upon the palms of My hands; your walls are continually before Me."

Isaiah 49:13,16

John saw the holy city, new Jerusalem, coming down from You, God, out of heaven. . . . You, God, will wipe away all tears from our eyes, and there will be no more death, nor sorrow, nor crying, neither shall there be any more pain, for the former things are passed away.

Revelation 21:2,4

You will swallow up death in victory, and You, Lord GOD, will wipe away tears from off all faces . . . for You, LORD, have spoken it.

Isaiah 25:8

Grief

I have called upon You, for You will hear me, O God. Incline Your ear to me and hear my speech. . . . Keep me as the apple of Your eye; hide me under the shadow of Your wings. . . . As for me, I will behold Your face in righteousness. I will be satisfied, when I awake, with Your likeness.

Psalm 17:6,8,15

You are blessed God, even the Father of my Lord Jesus Christ, Father of mercies and the God of all comfort, You comfort me in all my tribulation, that I may be able to comfort those who are in any trouble, by the comfort with which I myself am comforted by You.

2 Corinthians 1:3-4

Pleasure and pain are opposites:
when you share grief, you decrease it;
when you share joy, you increase it.

Unknown

A Teen Relies on God Regarding . . .

Illness

Heal me, O LORD, and I shall be healed. Save me, and I shall be saved, for You are my praise.

Jeremiah 17:14

The one who dwells in Your secret place, most High, will abide under the shadow of the Almighty. . . . There will no evil befall me, neither will any plague come near my dwelling.

Psalm 91:1,10

LORD, You open the eyes of the blind. You raise them up who are bowed down. You love the righteous.

Psalm 146:8

"Is any sick among you? Let that one call for the elders of the church, and let them pray over them, anointing them with oil in the name of the Lord. And the prayer of faith will save the sick, and the Lord shall raise them up."

James 5:14-15

You sent Your word and healed me and delivered me from their destruction.

Psalm 107:20

Illness

"Because you have set your love upon Me, therefore will I deliver you. I will set you on high, because you have known My name. . . . With long life will I satisfy you and show you My salvation."

Psalm 91:14,16

"My child, attend to my words; incline your ear to my sayings. Do not let them depart from your eyes. Keep them in the midst of your heart. For they are life to those who find them and health to all their flesh."

Proverbs 4:20-22

Though I walk through the valley of the shadow of death, I will fear no evil, for You are with me. Your rod and Your staff comfort me.

Psalm 23:4

Himself bore our sins in His own body on the tree so that we, being dead to sins, should live to righteousness. By His stripes we were healed.

1 Peter 2:24

ILLNESS

"If you will diligently hearken to the voice of the LORD your God and will do that which is right in His sight and will give ear to His commandments and keep all His statutes, I will put none of these diseases upon you, which I have brought upon the Egyptians, for I am the LORD who heals you."

Exodus 15:26

Bless the LORD, O my soul, and do not forget all His benefits, who forgives all my offenses, who heals all my diseases.

Psalm 103:2-3

"I was wounded for your transgressions, I was bruised for your offenses. The punishment for your peace was upon Me, and with My stripes you are healed."

Isaiah 53:5

Why are you downcast, O my soul? And why are you disquieted within me? Hope in God, for I will yet praise Him, who is the health of my countenance and my God.

Psalm 43:5

Illness

"To you who fear My name will the Sun of righteousness arise with healing in His wings; and you will go forth and grow up as a calves of the stall."

Malachi 4:2

LORD, You preserve the simple. I was brought low and You helped me. . . . I will walk before You, LORD, in the land of the living.

Psalm 116:6,9

I am blessed who considers the poor. You, LORD, will deliver me in time of trouble. You will preserve me and keep me alive, and I shall be blessed upon the earth, and You will not deliver me into the will of my enemies. LORD, You will strengthen me upon the bed of languishing. You will restore me on my bed of sickness.

Psalm 41:1-3

A merry heart does good like a medicine, but a broken spirit dries the bones.

Proverbs 17:22

Illness

"You shall serve Me, the LORD your God, and I shall bless your bread and your water, and I will take sickness away from your midst."

Exodus 23:25-26

God, You anointed Jesus of Nazareth with the Holy Spirit and with power, who went about doing good and healing all who were oppressed of the devil, for You were with Him.

Acts 10:38

A sound heart is the life of the flesh, but envy, the rottenness of the bones.

Proverbs 14:30

"O Israel, you have destroyed yourself, but in Me is your help. . . . I will ransom you from the power of the grave; I will redeem you from death. O death, I will be your plagues; O grave, I will be your destruction."

Hosea 13:9,14

How glorious to be able to tell each sick one, no matter what the disease from which they are suffering, that Christ has redeemed them from it.

Lilian B. Yeomans, M.D.

A Teen Relies on God Regarding . . .

Impure Thoughts

As one thinks in his heart, so is he.

Proverbs 23:7

Though we walk in the flesh, we do not war after the flesh. (For the weapons of our warfare are not carnal, but mighty through You, God, to the pulling down of strongholds;) casting down imaginations, and every high thing that exalts itself against the knowledge of You, God, and bringing into captivity every thought to the obedience of Christ.

2 Corinthians 10:3-5

"Present your bodies a living sacrifice, holy, acceptable to God, which is your reasonable service. And do not be conformed to this world, but be transformed by the renewing of your mind, that you may prove what is that good, and acceptable, and perfect, will of God."

Romans 12:1-3

IMPURE THOUGHTS

Wash me thoroughly from my evildoing, and cleanse me from my sin. For I acknowledge my transgressions, and my sin is ever before me. Against You, You only, have I sinned.

Psalm 51:2-4

[The apostle Paul wrote,] "Whatever things are . . . pure, . . . lovely, . . . if there be any virtue, and if there be any praise, think on these things. Those things, which you have both learned, and received, and heard, and seen in me, do, and the God of peace shall be with you."

Philippians 4:8-9

Your law, LORD, is perfect, converting my soul. . . . The fear of You, LORD, is clean, enduring forever.

Psalm 19:7,9

How shall a young person cleanse his way? By taking heed to it according to Your word. . . . Your word, LORD, have I hid in my heart, that I might not sin against You.

Psalm 119:9,11

Impure Thoughts

If I confess my sins, You are faithful and just to forgive me my sin, and to cleanse me from all unrighteousness.

1 John 1:9

I hate vain thoughts, but Your law do I love. You are my hiding place and my shield. I hope in Your word. . . . Uphold me according to Your word, that I may live. . . . Hold me up, and I shall be safe.

Psalm 119:113-114,116-117

Cleanse me from secret faults. Keep me, Your servant, back also from presumptuous sins. Do not let them have dominion over me. Then I shall be upright. . . . Let the words of my mouth, and the meditation of my heart, be acceptable in Your sight, O LORD, my strength, and my redeemer.

Psalm 19:12-14

Occupy your mind with good thoughts, or the enemy will fill it with bad ones: unoccupied it cannot be.

Sir Thomas More

Jealousy

The fear of You, LORD leads to life, and the one who has it will abide satisfied. He will not be visited with evil.

Proverbs 19:23

Godliness with contentment is great gain. For I brought nothing into this world, and it is certain I can carry nothing out.

1 Timothy 6:6-7

"'I will satisfy the soul of the priests with abundance, and My people shall be satisfied with My goodness,' says the LORD."

Jeremiah 31:14

"Let your character be without covetousness; and be content with the things you have, for He has said, 'I will never leave you nor forsake you.'"

Hebrews 13:5

"Do not let your heart envy sinners, but be in the fear of the LORD all day long. For surely there is a future, and your expectation will not be cut off."

Proverbs 23:17-18

Jealousy

You satisfy my mouth with good things so that my youth is renewed like the eagle's.

Psalm 103:5

Better is a handful with quietness, than both hands full with travail and annoyance.

Ecclesiastes 4:6

Because Your lovingkindness is better than life, my lips shall praise You. Thus I will bless You while I live. I will lift up my hands in Your name. My soul will be satisfied as with the best foods; and my mouth will praise You with joyful lips.

Psalm 63:3-5

"Rest in Me your LORD and wait patiently for Me. Do not fret because of the one who prospers in his way, because of the one who brings wicked devices to pass. . . . For evildoers will be cut off, but those who wait on the LORD shall inherit the earth."

Psalm 37:7,9

Jealousy

I who am Christ's have crucified the flesh with the affections and lusts. If I live in the Spirit, let me also walk in the Spirit. Let me not be conceited, provoking others, envying others.

Galatians 5:24-26

"Do not envy the oppressor, and do not choose any of his ways. For the perverse is an abomination to your LORD, but My secret is with the righteous."

Proverbs 3:31-32

If you have bitter envy and strife in your hearts, do not glory in it and do not lie against the truth. This wisdom does not descend from above, but is earthly, sensual, devilish.

James 3:14-15

Love does not envy.

1 Corinthians 13:4

A sound heart is the life of my flesh, but envy, rottenness to my bones.

Proverbs 14:30

And now, when any tempest-tossed soul fails to see that God is enough, I feel like saying, not with scorn, but with infinite pity, "Ah, dear friend, you do not know God! Did you know Him, you could not help seeing that He is the remedy for every need of your soul. . . . God is enough."

Hannah Whitall Smith

A Teen Relies on God Regarding . . .

Loneliness

Know that the LORD is God. It is He who has made us and not we ourselves; we are Your people and the sheep of Your pasture.

Psalm 100:3

"Look, I stand at the door and knock. If anyone hears My voice and opens the door, I will come into him and will eat with him and he with Me."

Revelation 3:20

"You are My friends if you do whatever I command you. From now on I do not call you servants, for the servant does not know what his lord does, but I have called you friends, for all things that I have heard of My Father I have made known to you. You have not chosen Me, but I have chosen you."

John 15:14-16

"I am with you always, even until the end of the world."

Matthew 28:20

LONELINESS

A father of the fatherless and a judge of the widows are You, God, in Your holy habitation. You set the solitary in families. You bring out those who are bound with chains, but the rebellious dwell in a dry land.

Psalm 68:5-6

Two are better than one, because they have a good reward for their labor. For if they fall, the one will lift up his fellow. But woe to him who is alone when he falls, for he does not have another to help him up. Again, if two lie together, then they have heat, but how can one be warm alone? And if one prevail against him, two shall withstand the one; and a threefold cord is not quickly broken.

Ecclesiastes 4:9-12

"I will not leave you comfortless. I will come to you."

John 14:18

LORD, You are good to those who wait for You, to the soul who seeks You.

Lamentations 3:25

Loneliness

LORD, You preserve the strangers; You relieve the fatherless and widow; but the way of the wicked You turn upside down.

Psalm 146:9

"Can a woman forget her sucking child, that she should not have compassion on the son of her womb? Yes, they may forget, yet I will not forget you. Look, I have engraved you on the palms of My hands; your walls are continually before Me."

Isaiah 49:15-16

You, my God, shall supply all my need according to Your riches in glory by Christ Jesus.

Philippians 4:19

You, LORD, are near to all who call on You, to all who call upon You in truth.

Psalm 145:18

One who has friends must show himself friendly, and there is a friend who sticks closer than a brother.

Proverbs 18:24

LONELINESS

"I will betroth you to Myself forever; yes, I will betroth you in righteousness, and in judgment, and in loving kindness, and in mercies. I will even betroth you to Myself in faithfulness, and you will know the LORD."

Hosea 2:19-20

He has said, "I will never leave you, nor forsake you."

Hebrews 13:5

"Draw near to Me, and I will draw near to you."

James 4:8

What man is he who fears You, LORD? He shall You teach in the way that he shall choose. His soul will dwell at ease, and his seed will inherit the earth.

Psalm 25:12-13

"'Come out from among them, and be separate,' says the Lord; 'and do not touch the unclean thing, and I will receive you, and will be a Father to you, and you will be My sons and daughters,' says the Lord Almighty."

2 Corinthians 6:17-18

Loneliness

"You will call and I, the Lord, will answer; you will cry, and I will say, 'Here I am.'"

Isaiah 58:9

I am complete in [Christ], who is the head of all principality and power.

Colossians 2:10

"Where two or three are gathered together in My name, I am there in the midst of them."

Matthew 18:20

My soul longs, yes, even faints for Your courts, Lord. My heart and my flesh cry out for You, the living God. . . . They are blessed who dwell in Your house. They will be ever praising You. . . . For a day in Your courts is better than a thousand. I had rather be a doorkeeper in Your house, God, than to dwell in the tents of wickedness.

Psalm 84:2,4,10

In silence and quiet the devout soul advances in virtue and learns the hidden truths of Scripture. There she finds a flood of tears with which to bathe and cleanse herself nightly, that she may become the more intimate with her Creator the farther she withdraws from all the tumult of the world.

Thomas á Kempis

A Teen Relies on God Regarding . . .

Loss

"I would not have you to be ignorant, fellow believers, concerning those who are asleep, that you not have sorrow, even as others who have no hope. For if we believe that Jesus died and rose again, even so those also who sleep in Jesus will God bring with Him."

1 Thessalonians 4:13-14

"The righteous perish and no one lays it to heart, and merciful people are taken away, none considering that the righteous is taken away from the evil to come. They shall enter into peace; they shall rest in their beds, each one walking in uprightness."

Isaiah 57:1-2

"The thief comes only to steal, kill, and destroy. I am come that you might have life and that you might have it more abundantly."

John 10:10

In the day of trouble I call upon You, for You will answer me.

Psalm 86:7

Loss

"I will restore to you the years that the locust has eaten . . . and you shall eat plenty and be satisfied and praise the name of the LORD your God who has dealt wondrously with you; and My people shall never be ashamed."

Joel 2:25-26

I am poor and sorrowful; let Your salvation, O God, set me up on high. I will praise Your name, God, with a song and will magnify You with thanksgiving. . . . The humble will see this and be glad. And my heart will live who seeks You, for You hear the poor.

Psalm 69:29-30,32-33

The sorrows of death surround me. . . . In my distress, I called upon You, LORD, and cried to You, my God. You heard my voice out of Your temple, and my cry came before You, into Your ears.

Psalm 18:4,6

Loss

O death, where is your sting? O grave, where is your victory? The sting of death is sin, and the strength of sin is the law. But thanks be to You, God, who gives me the victory through my Lord Jesus Christ.

1 Corinthians 15:55-57

"There is no one who has left house, or brothers, or sisters, or father, or mother, or wife, or children, or lands, for My sake, and the gospel's, but that person shall receive a hundredfold now in this time, houses, and brothers, and sisters, and mothers, and children, and lands, with persecutions; and in the world to come eternal life."

Mark 10:29-30

The wicked is driven away in his wickedness; but the righteous has hope [even] in death.

Proverbs 14:32

Faith draws the poison from every grief, takes the sting from every loss, and quenches the fire of every pain; and only faith can do it.

Josiah Gilbert Holland

A TEEN RELIES ON GOD REGARDING . . .

PEER PRESSURE

The fear of others brings a snare, but I put my trust in You, LORD, and I shall be safe.

Proverbs 29:25

Whoever keeps the law is a wise child, but the one who is a companion of riotous people shame their parents.

Proverbs 28:7

The one who walks with the wise shall be wise, but a companion of fools shall be destroyed. Evil pursues sinners, but to the righteous good shall be repaid.

Proverbs 13:20-21

"Do not be conformed to this world, but be transformed by the renewing of your mind, that you may prove what is My good, and acceptable, and perfect, will."

Romans 12:2

LORD, You are on my side; I will not fear. What can anyone do to me? Lord, You take my part with those who help me, therefore shall I see my desire upon those who hate me.

Psalm 118:6-7

Peer Pressure

A violent person entices his neighbor, and leads him into the way that is not good.

Proverbs 16:28

"'Come out from among them, and be separate,' says the Lord, 'and do not touch the unclean thing, and I will receive you, and will be a Father to you, and you will be My sons and daughters,' says the Lord Almighty."

2 Corinthians 6:17-18

I am a companion of all those who fear You, and of those who keep Your precepts. The earth, O LORD, is full of Your mercy. Teach me Your statutes.

Psalm 119:63

Those who rob their father or their mother, and say, "It is no transgression,"[those ones] are the companions of a destroyer.

Proverbs 28:24

The righteous are bold as a lion.

Proverbs 28:1

Fear of God can deliver us from the fear of man.

John Witherspoon

Pride

"Humble yourself in the sight of the Lord, and I will lift you up."

James 4:10

Before destruction the heart of a person is haughty, and before honor is humility.

Proverbs 18:12

All that is in the world, the lust of the flesh, and the lust of the eyes, and the pride of life, is not of You, Father, but is of the world. And the world passes away and the lust of it, but the one who does Your will God, abides forever.

1 John 2:16-17

You will save the afflicted people but will bring down high looks.

Psalm 18:27

Pride goes before destruction, and a haughty spirit before a fall. It is better [for me] to be of a humble spirit with the lowly, than to divide the spoil with the proud.

Proverbs 16:18-19

Pride

In the mouth of the foolish is a rod of pride, but the lips of the wise will preserve them.

Proverbs 14:3

When pride comes, then comes shame, but with the lowly is wisdom.

Proverbs 11:2

[Hannah prayed and said,] "Talk no more so exceeding proudly; do not let arrogance come out of your mouth, for the LORD is a God of knowledge, and by Him actions are weighed."

1 Samuel 2:3

With the merciful You will show Yourself merciful, and with the upright one You will show Yourself upright. With the pure You will show Yourself pure, and with the perverse You will show Yourself shrewd. And the afflicted people You will save, but Your eyes are upon the haughty, that You may bring them down.

2 Samuel 22:26-28

Things average out: if you think too much of yourself, other people won't.

Unknown

A TEEN RELIES ON GOD REGARDING . . .

PRIORITIES

"Seek first My kingdom, and My righteousness, and all these things will be added to you."

Matthew 6:33

"You shall love the Lord your God with all your heart, and with all your soul, and with all your mind, and with all your strength. This is the first commandment. And the second is like it: You shall love your neighbor as yourself. There is no other commandment greater than these."

Mark 12:30-31

"Children, obey your parents in the Lord, for this is right. Honor your father and mother; (which is the first commandment with promise;) that it may be well with you, and you may live long on the earth."

Ephesians 6:1-2

PRIORITIES

"Servants [employees], be obedient to those who are your masters [employers] according to the flesh, with fear and trembling, in singleness of your heart, as to Christ; not with eye service, as a people-pleaser; but as the servant of Christ, doing the will of God, from the heart; with good will doing service, as to the Lord, and not to people, knowing that whatever good thing anyone does, the same shall that one receive from the Lord."

Ephesians 6:5-8

"Honor everyone. Love fellow believers. Fear Me, your God. Honor the king [government officials]. Servants [employees], be subject to your masters [employers] with all fear, not only to the good and gentle, but also to the perverse. For this is thankworthy, if a person for conscience toward Me endures grief, suffering wrongfully."

1 Peter 2:17-19

"I, the LORD, the first, and the last; I am He."

Isaiah 41:4

Priorities

"'I am Alpha and Omega, the beginning and the last,' says the Lord, 'who is, and who was, and who is to come, the Almighty.'"

Revelation 1:8

The fear of You, LORD, is the beginning of wisdom. Good understanding have all who do Your commandments. Your praise endures forever.

Psalm 111:10

"Six days shall work be done, but the seventh day is the Sabbath of rest, a holy assembly. You shall do no work on it. It is the Sabbath of the LORD in all your dwellings."

Leviticus 23:3

Beloved, now are we the children of God, and it does not yet appear what we shall be; but we know that when He shall appear, we shall be like Him; for we shall see Him as He is. And every person that has this hope in them purifies themselves even as He is pure.

1 John 3:2-3

The Spirit of God alters my dominating desires; he alters the things that matter, and a universe of desires I had never known before suddenly comes on the horizon.

Oswald Chambers

A Teen Relies on God Regarding . . .

Rebellion

"'Come now, and let us reason together,' says the LORD. 'Though your sins are as scarlet, they shall be as white as snow. Though they are red like crimson, they shall be as wool. If you are willing and obedient, you shall eat the good of the land. But if you refuse and rebel, you shall be devoured with the sword, for the mouth of the LORD has spoken it.'"

Isaiah 1:18-20

"My sheep hear My voice, and I know them, and they follow Me. And I give to them eternal life, and they shall never perish, neither shall any man pluck them out of My hand. My Father, who gave them to me, is greater than all, and no one is able to pluck them out of My Father's hand."

John 10:27-29

Joy shall be in heaven over one sinner who repents.

Luke 15:7

Rebellion

"The servant of the Lord must not strive, but be gentle to all, apt to teach, patient, in meekness instructing those who oppose them, if God possibly will give them repentance to the acknowledging of the truth, and that they may recover themselves out of the snare of the devil, who are taken captive by him at his will."

2 Timothy 2:24-26

Surely He has born my griefs, and carried my sorrows. . . . He was wounded for my transgressions; He was bruised for my offenses.

Isaiah 53:4-5

It is You, God, who works in me both to will and to do of Your good pleasure.

Philippians 2:13

Your mercy, LORD, is from everlasting to everlasting upon those who fear You.

Psalm 103:17

Whom You love, LORD, You correct; even as a father the child in whom he delights.

Proverbs 3:12

Rebellion

"The son said to him, 'Father, I have sinned against heaven, and in your sight, and am no more worthy to be called your son.' But the father said to his servants, 'Bring the best robe, and put it on him, and put a ring on his hand, and shoes on his feet, and bring the fatted calf, and kill it, and let us eat, and be merry. For my son was dead, and is alive again; he was lost, and is found.'"

Luke 15:21-24

A wise child makes a glad father, but a foolish child is the mother's heaviness.

Proverbs 10:1

The rod and reproof give me wisdom, but children left to themselves bring their mother to shame.

Proverbs 29:15

"Walk worthy of Me, your God, who has called you to My kingdom and glory."

1 Thessalonians 2:12

"Repent, for the kingdom of heaven is at hand."

Matthew 3:2

REBELLION

The Lord is not slack concerning His promise . . . but is longsuffering toward me, not willing that any should perish [not even me], but that all should come to repentance.

2 Peter 3:9

"The Lord GOD says, 'Repent, and turn yourselves from all your transgressions, so evildoing shall not be your ruin.'"

Ezekiel 18:30-31

"Do you despise the riches of My goodness and forbearance and longsuffering, not knowing that My goodness leads you to repentance?"

Romans 2:4

"To obey is better than sacrifice. . . . Rebellion is as the sin of witchcraft, and stubbornness is as evildoing and idolatry."

1 Samuel 15:22-23

"The time is fulfilled, and the kingdom of God is at hand. Repent, and believe the gospel."

Mark 1:15

God will take nine steps toward us, but he will not take the tenth. He will incline us to repent, but he cannot do our repenting for us.

A.W. Tozer

A Teen Relies on God Regarding . . .

Rejection

My own familiar friend, in whom I trusted, who ate of my bread, has lifted up his heel against me. But You, O LORD, be merciful to me and raise me up, that I may repay them. By this I know that You favor me: because my enemy does not triumph over me.

Psalm 41:9-11

You are a gracious and merciful God . . . who keeps covenant and mercy.

Nehemiah 9:31-32

I will also be a crown of glory in the hand of the LORD, and a royal diadem in the hand of God. I shall no longer be called Forsaken; neither shall my land anymore be termed Desolate . . . for the LORD delights in me.

Isaiah 62:3-4

"You are blessed who are persecuted for righteousness' sake, for the kingdom of heaven is yours."

Matthew 5:10

Rejection

"If from now on you shall seek Me, the LORD your God, you will find Me, if you seek Me with all your heart and with all your soul. When you are in tribulation and all these things have come upon you, even in the latter days, if you turn to Me, the LORD your God, and will be obedient to My voice, (for the LORD your God, is a merciful God); I will not forsake you, neither destroy you, nor forget the covenant of your fathers which I swore to them."

Deuteronomy 4:29-31

I will call on You, LORD; who are worthy to be praised. So I will be saved from my enemies.

Psalm 18:3

"Do not let mercy and truth forsake you. Bind them around your neck; write them on the table of your heart, so you will find favor and good understanding in the sight of God and man."

Proverbs 3:3-4

"All who the Father gives Me will come to Me, and those who come to Me I will in no way cast out [not even you]."

John 6:37

Rejection

I have received the Spirit of adoption, by whom I cry, "Abba, Father." The Spirit Himself bears witness with my spirit that I am Your child, God.

Romans 8:15-16

"'I will restore health to you and I will heal you of your wounds,' says the LORD, 'because they called you an outcast.'"

Jeremiah 30:17

He is despised and rejected of men, a man of sorrows and acquainted with grief. . .. He was despised. . . . Surely He has borne my griefs and carried my sorrows. . . . He was wounded for my transgressions, He was bruised for my offenses. The punishment for my peace was upon Him, and with His stripes I am healed.

Isaiah 53:3-5

Fools make a mock at sin, but among the righteous there is favor.

Proverbs 14:9

Rejection

When one's ways please You, LORD, You make even his enemies to be at peace with him.

Proverbs 16:7

LORD, You will not cast off Your people, neither will You forsake Your inheritance.

Psalm 94:14

LORD, You will not forsake Your people for Your great name's sake, because it has pleased You to make us Your people.

1 Samuel 12:22

Let all who put their trust in You rejoice. Let them ever shout for joy, because You defend them. Let those also who love Your name be joyful in You. For You, LORD, will bless the righteous; You surround them with favor as with a shield.

Psalm 5:11-12

Although today he prunes my twigs with pain, Yet doth his blood nourish and warm my root; Tomorrow I shall put forth buds again And clothe myself with fruit.

Christina Georgina Rossetti

A Teen Relies on God Regarding . . .

Selfishness

"Give and it will be given to you—good measure, pressed down, shaken together, and running over, will be given to you."

Luke 6:38

"No good thing will I withhold from You who walk uprightly."

Psalm 84:11

"Is not this the fast that I have chosen? . . . Is it not to give your bread to the hungry, and that you bring the poor who are cast out to your house? when you see the naked, that you cover them; and that you not hide yourself from your own relatives? Then shall your light break forth as the morning, and your health shall spring forth speedily: and your righteousness shall go before you; the glory of the LORD shall be your reward. Then shall you call, and the LORD shall answer; you shall cry, and He shall say, 'Here I am.'"

Isaiah 58:6-9

Selfishness

Whoever has pity on the poor lends to You, LORD, and that which one has given will You pay [the giver] again.

Proverbs 19:17

"Since you have done it to one of the least of these My brothers, you have done it to Me."

Matthew 25:40

"Whoever will be great among you, shall be your minister, and whoever of you will be the first, shall be servant of all. For even the Son of man did not come to be ministered to, but to minister, and to give His life a ransom for many."

Mark 10:43-45

The one who gives to the poor shall not lack, but the one who hides his eyes shall have many curses.

Proverbs 28:27

The one who has a bountiful eye shall be blessed, for he gives of his bread to the poor.

Proverbs 22:9

If I really love God, my innate and persistent selfishness will have received its death-blow.

Alexander Smellie

A Teen Relies on God Regarding . . .

Self-Pity

In the day of my trouble I sought You, Lord. My sore ran in the night, and did not cease. My soul refused to be comforted. I remembered You, God, and was troubled. I complained, and my spirit was overwhelmed. . . . I call to remembrance my song in the night; I commune with my own heart. . . . I will remember Your works, LORD. . . . I will meditate also on all Your work, and talk of Your doing. . . . Who is so great a God as our God? You are the God who does wonders. You have declared Your strength among the people.

Psalm 77:2-3,6,11-14

Building up yourselves on your most holy faith, praying in the Holy Spirit, keep yourselves in the love of God, looking for the mercy of our Lord Jesus Christ to eternal life.

Jude 20-21

"Do not cast away, therefore, your confidence, which has great recompense of reward."

Hebrews 10:35

Self-pity

Bless the LORD, O my soul, and all that is within me, bless His holy name. Bless the LORD, O my soul, and forget not all His benefits; who forgives all my offenses; who heals all my diseases; who redeems my life from destruction; who crowns me with lovingkindness and tender mercies; who satisfies my mouth with good things; so that my youth is renewed like the eagle's.

Psalm 103:1-5

I will lift up my eyes to the hills, where my help comes from. My help comes from You, LORD, who made heaven and earth.

Psalm 121:1-2

I come boldly to Your throne of grace, that I may obtain mercy, and find grace to help in time of need.

Hebrews 4:16

I felt sorry for myself because I had no shoes—
until I met a man who had no feet.

Unknown

A Teen Relies on God Regarding . . .

Shame

They looked to You and were lightened, and their faces were not ashamed. This poor person cried, and You, LORD, heard me and saved me out of all my troubles.

Psalm 34:5-6

If we walk in the light as He is in the light, we have fellowship one with another and the blood of Jesus Christ His Son cleanses us from all sin.

1 John 1:7

I am poor and needy, yet You, Lord, think about me. You are my help and my deliverer; do not delay, O my God.

Psalm 40:17

With the pure, You will show Yourself pure; and with the distorted, You will show Yourself shrewd. For You will save the afflicted people, but will bring down high looks. For You will light my candle. You, the LORD my God, will enlighten my darkness.

Psalm 18:26-28

Shame

I am the temple of the living God, as You have said, "I will dwell in them and walk in them; and I will be their God, and they will be my people." . . . Having Your promises, I cleanse myself from all filthiness of the flesh and spirit, perfecting holiness in the fear of You, God.

2 Corinthians 6:16, 7:1

To me was granted that I should be arrayed in fine linen, clean and white, for fine linen is the righteousness of saints.

Revelation 19:8

Christ loved the church [which includes me] and gave Himself for it, that He might sanctify and cleanse it with the washing of water by the word, that He might present it to Himself a glorious church, not having spot or wrinkle or any such thing, but that it should be holy and without blemish.

Ephesians 5:25-27

Shame

"I will sprinkle clean water upon you, and you will be clean; from all your filthiness and from all your idols, I will cleanse you. A new heart also will I give you, and a new spirit will I put within you; and I will take away the stony heart out of your flesh, and I will give you a heart of flesh. And I will put My Spirit within you and cause you to walk in My statutes, and you will keep my judgments and do them. . . . I will also save you from all your uncleanness."

Ezekiel 36:25-27,29

"I will cleanse them from all their evildoing, by which they have sinned against Me; and I will pardon all their offenses, by which they have sinned and by which they have transgressed against Me."

Jeremiah 33:8

[Jesus said,] "Now you are clean through the word which I have spoken to you."

John 15:3

Shame

Truly You are good to Israel, even to such as are of a clean heart.

Psalm 73:1

The fear of You, LORD, is clean, enduring forever; Your judgments are true and righteous altogether.

Psalm 19:9

The king's favor is toward a wise servant, but his wrath is against him who causes shame.

Proverbs 14:35

Purge me with hyssop, and I will be clean. Wash me, and I will be whiter than snow.

Psalm 51:7

"They shall not defile themselves anymore with their idols, nor with their detestable things, nor with any of their transgressions. But I will save them out of all their dwelling places, in which they have sinned, and will cleanse them, so they will be My people, and I will be their God."

Ezekiel 37:23

SHAME

"The LORD your God in the midst of you is mighty; He will save, He will rejoice over you with joy; He will rest in His love, He will joy over you with singing. I will gather those who are sorrowful for the solemn assembly, who are of you to whom the reproach of it was a burden. Look, at that time I will undo all who afflict you, and I will save the one who halts and gather the one who was driven out; and I will get them praise and fame in every land where they have been put to shame."

Zephaniah 3:17-19

[LORD,] draw near to my soul and redeem it. Deliver me because of my enemies. You have known my reproach, and my shame, and my dishonor. My adversaries are all before You.

Psalm 69:18-19

A gracious woman retains honor, and strong men retain riches.

Proverbs 11:16

Shame

"Sanctify yourselves therefore, and be holy, for I am the LORD your God. And you shall keep My statutes and do them. I am the LORD who sanctifies you."

Leviticus 20:7-8

The Scripture says, "Whoever believes on Him will not be ashamed."

Romans 10:11

Then I will not be ashamed, when I have respect for all Your commandments. . . . How shall a young person cleanse their way? By taking heed to it according to Your word.

Psalm 119:6,9

It is written, "Look, I lay in Zion a stumblingstone and a rock of offense, and whoever believes on Him shall not be ashamed."

Romans 9:33

For sin has played many evil tricks upon us, and one has been the infusing into us a false sense of shame. There is hardly a man or woman who dares to be just what he or she is without doctoring up the impression. The fear of being found out gnaws like rodents within their hearts.

W. Tozer

A Teen Relies on God Regarding . . .

Stress

"We would not, fellow believers, have you ignorant of our trouble which came to us in Asia, that we were pressed out of measure, above strength, so much so that we despaired even of life. But we had the sentence of death in ourselves, that we should not trust in ourselves, but in God who raises the dead, who delivered us from so great a death and does deliver, in whom we trust that He will yet deliver us."

2 Corinthians 1:8-10

"Come to me, all you who labor and are heavy laden, and I will give you rest. Take My yoke upon you, and learn of Me, for I am meek and lowly in heart, and you will find rest for your souls. For My yoke is easy, and My burden is light."

Matthew 11:28-30

Stress

You give power to the faint; and to those who have no might, You increase strength.

Isaiah 40:29

They cry to You, LORD, in their trouble, and You bring them out of their distresses. You make the storm calm so that the waves are still. Then they are glad because they [the waves] are quiet, so You bring them to their desired haven.

Psalm 107:28-30

Even the youths will faint and be weary, and the young men will utterly fall, but those who wait on You, LORD, shall renew their strength. They shall mount up with wings as eagles; they will run and not be weary, and they shall walk and not faint.

Isaiah 40:30-31

When I said, "My foot slips," Your mercy, O LORD, held me up. In the multitude of my thoughts within me, Your comforts delight my soul.

Psalm 94:18-19

Stress

"Be still and know that I am God. I will be exalted among the heathen; I will be exalted in the earth." The LORD of hosts is with me; the God of Jacob is my refuge.

Psalm 46:10-11

[Jesus] arose and rebuked the wind and said to the sea, "Peace, be still." And the wind ceased, and there was a great calm. And He said to them, "Why are you so fearful? How is it that you have no faith?" And they feared exceedingly and said to one another, "What manner of man is this that even the wind and the sea obey Him?"

Mark 4:39-41

God is a tranquil being and abides in a tranquil eternity. So must your spirit become a tranquil and clear little pool, wherein the serene light of God can be mirrored.

Gerhard Tersteegen

Temptation

You are able to keep me from falling and to present me faultless before the presence of Your glory with exceeding joy.

Jude 24

"I [God] give more grace. Which is why I say, 'I resist the proud but give grace to the humble.' Submit yourself, therefore, to Me. Resist the devil, and he will flee from you."

James 4:6-7

You, Lord, know how to deliver the godly out of temptations.

2 Peter 2:9

"Let the one who thinks they stand take heed lest they fall. There is no temptation taken you but such as is common to people, but I am faithful, who will not allow you to be tempted above what you are able, but will with the temptation also make a way to escape, that you may be able to bear it."

1 Corinthians 10:12-13

Temptation

Count it all joy when you fall into various temptations, knowing that the trying of your faith works patience. But let patience have her perfect work, that you may be perfect and entire, wanting nothing. . . . Blessed is the one who endures temptation, for when he is tried, he will receive the crown of life, which the Lord has promised to those who love Him.

James 1:2-4,12

I am of You, God, and have overcome them [false spirits and prophets], because greater is He that is in me, than he that is in the world.

1 John 4:4

Sin shall not have dominion over me, for I am not under the law but under grace.

Romans 6:14

"Do not be wise in your own eyes. Fear Me, your LORD, and depart from evil. It will be health to your navel and nourishment to your bones."

Proverbs 3:7-8

TEMPTATION

I do not have a high priest who cannot be touched with the feeling of my infirmities; but He was in all points tempted like I am, yet without sin. I therefore come boldly to the throne of grace, that I may obtain mercy and find grace to help in time of need.

Hebrews 4:15-16

You who love the LORD, hate evil. He preserves the souls of His saints; He delivers them out of the hand of the wicked.

Psalm 97:10

God, You are my refuge and strength, a very present help in trouble.

Psalm 46:1

In that [Jesus] Himself has suffered being tempted, He is able to help those [like me] who are tempted.

Hebrews 2:18

"Keep your heart with all diligence, for out of it are the issues of life."

Proverbs 4:23

Your word have I hidden in my heart, that I might not sin against You. Blessed are You, O LORD.

Psalm 119:10-11

Temptation

Have mercy on me, O God, according to Your lovingkindness. According to the multitude of Your tender mercies, blot out my transgressions. Wash me thoroughly from my evildoing, and cleanse me from my sin. For I acknowledge my transgressions, and my sin is ever before me. . . . Behold, You desire truth in the inward parts; and in the hidden part You will make me to know wisdom.

Psalm 51:1-3,6

"Let no one say when they are tempted, 'I am tempted of God,' for I, God, cannot be tempted with evil, neither do I tempt anyone. But every person is tempted, when they are drawn away of their own lust and enticed."

James 1:13-14

My eyes are ever toward You, LORD; for You shall pluck my feet out of the net. . . . Let integrity and uprightness preserve me, for I wait on You.

Psalm 25:15,21

TEMPTATION

Who can understand his errors? LORD, cleanse me from secret faults. Keep back Your servant also from presumptuous sins; do not let them have dominion over me. Then I will be upright, and I will be innocent from the great transgression.

Psalm 19:12-13

When wisdom enters into my heart and knowledge is pleasant to my soul, discretion will preserve me, understanding will keep me, to deliver me from the way of the evil man, from the one who speaks perverse things, who leaves the paths of uprightness to walk in the ways of darkness . . . to deliver me from the strange woman, even from the stranger who flatters with her words, who forsakes the guide of her youth and forgets the covenant of her God.

Proverbs 2:10-13,16-17

Temptation is the devil looking through the keyhole; yielding is opening the door and inviting him in.

Billy Sunday

A Teen Relies on God Regarding . . .

Worry

"Do not worry about anything, but in everything by prayer and supplication with thanksgiving let your requests be made known to Me. And My peace, which passes all understanding, will keep your hearts and minds through Christ Jesus."

Philippians 4:6-7

Where no counsel is, the people fall; but in the multitude of counselors, there is safety.

Proverbs 11:14

I will hear what You, God the LORD, will speak, for You will speak peace to Your people and to Your saints. But do not let them turn to folly again.

Psalm 85:8

I will both lay myself down in peace and sleep, for You only, LORD, make me dwell in safety.

Psalm 4:8

Be diligent to make your calling and election sure, for if you do these things, you will never fall.

2 Peter 1:10

Worry

You have also given me the shield of Your salvation. Your right hand has held me up, and Your gentleness has made me great. You have enlarged my steps under me, so that my feet did not slip.

Psalm 18:35-36

God, You are my salvation. I will trust and not be afraid, for You, the LORD JEHOVAH, are my strength and my song. You also are become my salvation.

Isaiah 12:2

God, You have not given me the spirit of fear but of power, and of love, and of a sound mind.

2 Timothy 1:7

"My child, do not let [wisdom and understanding] depart from your eyes; keep sound wisdom and discretion. . . . When you lie down, you will not be afraid. Yes, you will lie down, and your sleep will be sweet."

Proverbs 3:21,24

"Humble yourself . . . casting all your care on Me, for I care for you."

1 Peter 5:6-7

Worry

"Take no thought, saying What will we eat? Or, What will we drink? Or, With what will we be clothed? . . . for your heavenly Father knows that you have need of all these things. But seek first the kingdom of God and His righteousness, and all these things will be added to you."

Matthew 6:31-33

Blessed is the one who trusts in You, LORD, and whose hope You are. For they will be as a tree planted by the waters, and that spreads out her roots by the river, and shall not fear when heat comes, but her leaf will be green, and will not be full of care in the year of drought, neither shall cease from yielding fruit.

Jeremiah 17:7-8

Your word is a lamp to my feet and a light to my path.

Psalm 119:105

I am an old man and have known a great many troubles, but most of them never happened.

Mark Twain

31 Scripture Affirmations for a Transformed You

Faith is an affirmation and an act
That bids eternal truth be fact.
Samuel Taylor Coleridge

Don't let the world around you squeeze you into its mould, but let God re-make you so that your whole attitude of mind is changed. Thus you will prove in practice that the will of God is good, acceptable to him and perfect.

Romans 12:2 PHILLIPS

Personal Affirmations for
Your Day

DAY 1

God, You did not send Your Son into the world to condemn me, but so that through Him I might be saved.

John 3:17

DAY 2

God, it is You who works in me both to will and to do of Your good pleasure.

Philippians 2:13

DAY 3

God, I know that all things work together for my good because I love You and am called according to Your purpose.

Romans 8:28

DAY 4

God, You have not given me the spirit of fear but of power, of love, and of a sound mind.

2 Timothy 1:7

DAY 5

If I lack wisdom, God, let me ask You for it. You give liberally to me, and You do not reprimand me for asking. And it shall be given to me.

James 1:5

YOUR DAY

DAY 6

I sought You, LORD, and You heard me, and delivered me from all my fears.

Psalm 34:4

DAY 7

I do not fear for You are with me. I am not dismayed for You are my God. You will strengthen me; yes, You will help me; yes, You will uphold me with the right hand of Your righteousness.

Isaiah 41:10

DAY 8

If I confess my sins, You are faithful and just to forgive me of my sins and to cleanse me from all unrighteousness.

1 John 1:9

DAY 9

Bless the LORD, O my soul, and do not forget His benefits. He forgives all my offenses; He heals all my diseases.

Psalm 103:2-3

DAY 10

This is the confidence that I have in [Christ]: if I ask anything according to His will, He hears me; and if I know that He hears me, whatever I ask, I know that I have the petitions that I desire of Him.

1 John 5:14-15

DAY 11

Who is the one who condemns me? It is Christ who died, yes, rather, that is risen again, who is even at Your right hand, God, who also makes intercession for me.

Romans 8:34

DAY 12

Peace Jesus leaves with me, His peace He gives to me. He does not give to me as the world gives. I do not let my heart be troubled, nor do I let it be afraid.

John 14:27

DAY 13

I am confident of this very thing, that You who have begun a good work in me will perform it until the day of Jesus Christ.

Philippians 1:6

DAY 14

LORD, You are my light and my salvation. Whom shall I fear? You are the strength of my life. Of whom shall I be afraid?

Psalm 27:1

DAY 15

You will keep me in perfect peace whose mind is fixed on You, because I trust in You.

Isaiah 26:3

DAY 16

LORD, You will show me the path of life. In Your presence is fullness of joy. At Your right hand there are pleasures forever.

Psalm 16:11

DAY 17

You are my God and You shall supply all my need according to Your riches in glory by Christ Jesus.

Philippians 4:19

DAY 18

Christ has redeemed me from the curse of the law, being made a curse for me, for it is written, "Cursed is everyone who hangs on a tree." He did this so that the blessing of Abraham might come on me through Jesus Christ, that I might receive the promise of the Spirit through faith.

Galatians 3:13-14

DAY 19

LORD, You are my Redeemer, the Holy One of Israel. You are the LORD my God, who teaches me to profit and leads me by the way that I should go.

Isaiah 48:17

DAY 20

I cast all of my care upon You, God, for You care for me.

1 Peter 5:7

DAY 21

If I abide in Christ and His words abide in me, I shall ask whatever I wish, and it shall be done for me.

John 15:7

DAY 22

LORD, You have turned my mourning into dancing. You have put off my mourning clothes and surrounded me with gladness.

Psalm 30:11

DAY 23

Give and it will be given to me—good measure, pressed down, shaken together, and running over, will men give to me. For with the same measure that I use, it shall be measured to me as well.

Luke 6:38

DAY 24

God, I am Your workmanship, created in Christ Jesus for good works, which You have before ordained that I should walk in them.

Ephesians 2:10

DAY 25

God, You are able to do exceedingly abundantly above all that I ask or think, according to the power that works in me.

Ephesians 3:20

DAY 26

Because I drink of the water that Jesus give me, I shall never thirst; but the water that Jesus gives shall be in me a well of water springing up into everlasting life.

John 4:14

DAY 27

Now there is no condemnation to me who is in Christ Jesus and who does not walk after the flesh but after the Spirit.

Romans 8:1

DAY 28

By grace I am saved through faith, and it is not of myself; it is Your gift, God.

Ephesians 2:8

DAY 29

I acknowledged my sin to You, and I have not hidden my evildoing. I said, I will confess my transgressions to the LORD; and You forgave the iniquity of my sin.

Psalm 32:5

DAY 30

Whatever things I desire, when I pray, I believe that I receive them and I shall have them.

Mark 11:24

DAY 31

Faithful are You who has called me; You also will do it.

1 Thessalonians 5:24

Classic Bible Passages for Meditation

*I*n coming to the Lord by means of "praying the Scripture," you do not read quickly; you read very slowly. You do not move from one passage to another, not until you have sensed the very heart of what you have read. You may than want to take that portion of Scripture that has touched you and turn it into prayer . . . Of course, there is a kind of reading the Scripture for scholarship and for study—but not here. . . . You are seeking to find the Lord in what you are reading . . . to take everything from the passage that unveils the Lord to you.

Madame Jeanne Guyon

Do not let this Book of the Law depart from your mouth; meditate on it day and night, so that you may be careful to do everything written in it. Then you will be prosperous and successful.

Joshua 1:8 NIV

The Ten Commandments

Then God spoke all these words:

"I am the Lord your God, who brought you out of the land of Egypt where you were slaves.

"You must not have any other gods except me.

"You must not make for yourselves an idol that looks like anything in the sky above or on the earth below or in the water below the land. You must not worship or serve any idol, because I, the Lord your God, am a jealous God. If you hate me, I will punish your children, and even your grandchildren and great-grandchildren. But I show kindness to thousands who love me and obey my commands.

"You must not use the name of the Lord your God thoughtlessly; the Lord will punish anyone who misuses his name.

The Ten Commandments

"Remember to keep the Sabbath holy. Work and get everything done during six days each week, but the seventh day is a day of rest to honor the Lord your God. On that day no one may do any work: not you, your son or daughter, your male or female slaves, your animals, or the foreigners living in your cities. The reason is that in six days the Lord made everything—the sky, the earth, the sea, and everything in them. On the seventh day he rested. So the Lord blessed the Sabbath day and made it holy.

"Honor your father and your mother so that you will live a long time in the land that the Lord your God is going to give you.

"You must not murder anyone.

"You must not be guilty of adultery.

"You must not steal.

"You must not tell lies about your neighbor.

"You must not want to take your neighbor's house. You must not want his wife or his male or female slaves, or his ox or his donkey, or anything that belongs to your neighbor."

Exodus 20:1-17 NCV

A Life of Blessing

Blessed is the man
who does not walk in the counsel of the wicked
or stand in the way of sinners
or sit in the seat of mockers.
But his delight is in the law of the LORD,
and on his law he meditates day and night.
He is like a tree planted by streams of water,
which yields its fruit in season
and whose leaf does not wither.
Whatever he does prospers.
Not so the wicked!
They are like chaff
that the wind blows away.
Therefore the wicked will not stand in
  the judgment,
nor sinners in the assembly of the righteous.
For the LORD watches over the way of
  the righteous,
but the way of the wicked will perish.

Psalm 1 NIV

Prayer of Repentance

God, be merciful to me
because you are loving.
Because you are always ready to be merciful,
wipe out all my wrongs.
Wash away all my guilt
and make me clean again.
I know about my wrongs,
and I can't forget my sin.
You are the only one I have sinned against;
I have done what you say is wrong.
You are right when you speak
and fair when you judge.
I was brought into this world in sin.
In sin my mother gave birth to me.
You want me to be completely truthful,
so teach me wisdom.
Take away my sin, and I will be clean.
Wash me, and I will be whiter than snow.
Make me hear sounds of joy and gladness;
let the bones you crushed be happy again.
Turn your face from my sins
and wipe out all my guilt.

PRAYER OF REPENTANCE

Create in me a pure heart, God,
and make my spirit right again.
Do not send me away from you
or take your Holy Spirit away from me.
Give me back the joy of your salvation.
Keep me strong by giving me a willing spirit.
Then I will teach your ways to those who
do wrong,
and sinners will turn back to you.
God, save me from the guilt of murder,
God of my salvation,
and I will sing about your goodness.
Lord, let me speak
so I may praise you.
You are not pleased by sacrifices, or I would
give them.
You don't want burnt offerings.
The sacrifice God wants is a broken spirit.
God, you will not reject a heart that is broken and
sorry for sin.

Psalm 51:1-17 NCV

The Lord Is Your Protection

He who dwells in the shelter of the Most High
Will abide in the shadow of the Almighty.
I will say to the LORD, "My refuge and
my fortress,
My God, in whom I trust!"
For it is He who delivers you from the snare of
the trapper
And from the deadly pestilence.
He will cover you with His pinions,
And under His wings you may seek refuge;
His faithfulness is a shield and bulwark.
You will not be afraid of the terror by night,
Or of the arrow that flies by day;
Of the pestilence that stalks in darkness,
Or of the destruction that lays waste at noon.
A thousand may fall at your side
And ten thousand at your right hand,
But it shall not approach you.
You will only look on with your eyes
And see the recompense of the wicked.

The Lord Is Your Protection

For you have made the LORD, my refuge,
Even the Most High, your dwelling place.
No evil will befall you,
Nor will any plague come near your tent.
For He will give His angels charge concerning you,
To guard you in all your ways.
They will bear you up in their hands,
That you do not strike your foot against a stone.
You will tread upon the lion and cobra,
The young lion and the serpent you will
trample down.
"Because he has loved Me, therefore I will
deliver him;
I will set him *securely* on high, because he has
known My name.
"He will call upon Me, and I will answer him;
I will be with him in trouble;
I will rescue him and honor him.
"With a long life I will satisfy him
And let him see My salvation."

Psalm 91 NASB

THE LORD SEARCHES AND KNOWS ME

O Lord, you have examined my heart and know everything about me. You know when I sit or stand. When far away you know my every thought. You chart the path ahead of me, and tell me where to stop and rest. Every moment, you know where I am. You know what I am going to say before I even say it. You both precede and follow me, and place your hand of blessing on my head.

This is too glorious, too wonderful to believe! I can *never be* lost to your Spirit! I can *never* get away from my God! If I go up to heaven, you are there; if I go down to the place of the dead, you are there. If I ride the morning winds to the farthest oceans, even there your hand will guide me, your strength will support me. If I try to hide in the darkness, the night becomes light around me. For even darkness cannot hide from God; to you the night shines as bright as day. Darkness and light are both alike to you.

The Lord Searches and Knows Me

You made all the delicate, inner parts of my body, and knit them together in my mother's womb. Thank you for making me so wonderfully complex! It is amazing to think about. Your workmanship is marvelous—and how well I know it. You were there while I was being formed in utter seclusion! You saw me before I was born and scheduled each day of my life before I began to breathe. Every day was recorded in your Book!

How precious it is, Lord, to realize that you are thinking about me constantly! I can't even count how many times a day your thoughts turn towards me. And when I waken in the morning, you are still thinking of me! . . .

Search me, O God, and know my heart; test my thoughts. Point out anything you find in me that makes you sad, and lead me along the path of everlasting life.

Psalm 139:1-18,23-24 TLB

GOD'S WAYS ARE HIGHER

Let the wicked forsake their way,
and the unrighteous their thoughts;
let them return to the Lord, that he may have mercy
on them,
and to our God, for he will abundantly pardon.

For my thoughts are not your thoughts,
nor are your ways my ways, says the Lord.
For as the heavens are higher than the earth,
so are my ways higher than your ways
and my thoughts than your thoughts.
For as the rain and the snow come down from heaven,
and do not return there until they have watered
the earth,
making it bring forth and sprout,
giving seed to the sower and bread to the eater,
so shall my word be that goes out from my mouth;
it shall not return to me empty,
but it shall accomplish that which I purpose,
and succeed in the thing for which I sent it.

Isaiah 55:7-11 NRSV

The Beatitudes

When Jesus saw the crowds, He went up on the mountain; and after He sat down, His disciples came to Him. He opened His mouth and *began* to teach them, saying,

"Blessed are the poor in spirit, for theirs is the kingdom of heaven.

"Blessed are those who mourn, for they shall be comforted.

"Blessed are the gentle, for they shall inherit the earth.

"Blessed are those who hunger and thirst for righteousness, for they shall be satisfied.

"Blessed are the merciful, for they shall receive mercy.

"Blessed are the pure in heart, for they shall see God.

"Blessed are the peacemakers, for they shall be called sons of God.

"Blessed are those who have been persecuted for the sake of righteousness, for theirs is the kingdom of heaven.

"Blessed are you when *people* insult you and persecute you, and falsely say all kinds of evil against you because of Me.

"Rejoice and be glad, for your reward in heaven is great; for in the same way they persecuted the prophets who were before you."

Matthew 5:1-12 NASB

Love Your Enemies

"You have heard that it was said, 'Love your neighbor and hate your enemy.' But I tell you: Love your enemies and pray for those who persecute you, that you may be sons of your Father in heaven. He causes his sun to rise on the evil and the good, and sends rain on the righteous and the unrighteous. If you love those who love you, what reward will you get? Are not even the tax collectors doing that? And if you greet only your brothers, what are you doing more than others? Do not even pagans do that? Be perfect, therefore, as your heavenly Father is perfect."

Matthew 5:43-48 NIV

THE LORD'S PRAYER

"In this manner, therefore, pray:

Our Father in heaven,
Hallowed be Your name.
Your kingdom come.
Your will be done
On earth as *it is* in heaven.
Give us this day our daily bread.
And forgive us our debts,
As we forgive our debtors.
And do not lead us into temptation,
But deliver us from the evil one.
For Yours is the kingdom and the power and
the glory forever. Amen.

"For if you forgive men their trespasses, your heavenly Father will also forgive you. But if you do not forgive men their trespasses, neither will your Father forgive your trespasses."

Matthew 6:9-15 NKJV

Love Is . . .

If I speak with human eloquence and angelic ecstasy but don't love, I'm nothing but the creaking of a rusty gate.

If I speak God's Word with power, revealing all his mysteries and making everything plain as day, and if I have faith that says to a mountain, "Jump," and it jumps, but I don't love, I'm nothing.

If I give everything I own to the poor and even go to the stake to be burned as a martyr, but I don't love, I've gotten nowhere. So, no matter what I say, what I believe, and what I do, I'm bankrupt without love.

Love never gives up.

Love cares more for others than for self.

Love Is . . .

Love doesn't want what it doesn't have.
Love doesn't strut,
Doesn't have a swelled head,
Doesn't force itself on others,
Isn't always "me first,"
Doesn't fly off the handle,
Doesn't keep score of the sins of others,
Doesn't revel when others grovel,
Takes pleasure in the flowering of truth,
Puts up with anything,
Trusts God always,
Always looks for the best,
Never looks back,
But keeps going to the end.

Love never dies. Inspired speech will be over some day; praying in tongues will end; understanding will reach its limit. We know only a portion of the truth, and what we say about God is always incomplete. But when the Complete arrives, our incompletes will be canceled.

Love Is . . .

When I was an infant at my mother's breast, I gurgled and cooed like any infant. When I grew up, I left those infant ways for good.

We don't yet see things clearly. We're squinting in a fog, peering through a mist. But it won't be long before the weather clears and the sun shines bright! We'll see it all then, see it all as clearly as God sees us, knowing him directly just as he knows us!

But for right now, until that completeness, we have three things to do to lead us toward that consummation: Trust steadily in God, hope unswervingly, love extravagantly. And the best of the three is love.

1 Corinthians 13:1-13 THE MESSAGE

THE ARMOR OF GOD

Be strong with the Lord's mighty power. Put on all of God's armor so that you will be able to stand firm against all strategies and tricks of the Devil. For we are not fighting against people made of flesh and blood, but against the evil rulers and authorities of the unseen world, against those mighty powers of darkness who rule this world, and against wicked spirits in the heavenly realms.

Use every piece of God's armor to resist the enemy in the time of evil, so that after the battle you will still be standing firm. Stand your ground, putting on the sturdy belt of truth and the body armor of God's righteousness. For shoes, put on the peace that comes from the Good News, so that you will be fully prepared. In every battle you will need faith as your shield to stop the fiery arrows aimed at you by Satan. Put on salvation as your helmet, and take the sword of the Spirit, which is the word of God. Pray at all times and on every occasion in the power of the Holy Spirit. Stay alert and be persistent in your prayers for all Christians everywhere.

Ephesians 6:10-18 NLT

WALKING IN THE LIGHT

This is the message we have heard from Him and announce to you, that God is Light, and in Him there is no darkness at all. If we say that we have fellowship with Him and *yet* walk in the darkness, we lie and do not practice the truth; but if we walk in the Light as He Himself is in the Light, we have fellowship with one another, and the blood of Jesus His Son cleanses us from all sin. If we say that we have no sin, we are deceiving ourselves and the truth is not in us. If we confess our sins, He is faithful and righteous to forgive us our sins and to cleanse us from all unrighteousness. If we say that we have not sinned, we make Him a liar and His word is not in us.

1 John 1:5-10 NASB

Think on These Things

Do not fret *or* have any anxiety about anything, but in every circumstance *and* in everything, by prayer and petition (definite requests), with thanksgiving, continue to make your wants known to God. And God's peace [shall be yours, that tranquil state of a soul assured of its salvation through Christ, and so fearing nothing from God and being content with its earthly lot of whatever sort that is, that peace] which transcends all understanding shall garrison *and* mount guard over your hearts and minds in Christ Jesus.

For the rest, brethren, whatever is true, whatever is worthy of reverence *and* is honorable *and* seemly, whatever is just, whatever is pure, whatever is lovely *and* lovable, whatever is kind *and* winsome *and* gracious, if there is any virtue *and* excellence, if there is anything worthy of praise, think on *and* weigh *and* take account of these things [fix your minds on them]. Practice what you have learned and received and heard and seen in me, *and* model your way of living on it, and the God of peace (of untroubled, undisturbed well-being) will be with you.

Philippians 4:6-9 AMP

A New Heaven and a New Earth

Now I saw a new heaven and a new earth, for the first heaven and the first earth had passed away. Also there was no more sea. Then I, John, saw the holy city, New Jerusalem, coming down out of heaven from God, prepared as a bride adorned for her husband. And I heard a loud voice from heaven saying, "Behold, the tabernacle of God *is* with men, and He will dwell with them, and they shall be His people. God Himself will be with them *and be* their God. And God will wipe away every tear from their eyes; there shall be no more death, nor sorrow, nor crying. There shall be no more pain, for the former things have passed away."

Revelation 21:1-4 NKJV

A loving Personality dominates the Bible, walking among the trees of the garden and breathing fragrance over every scene. Always a living Person is present, speaking, pleading, loving, working, and manifesting himself whenever and wherever his people have the receptivity necessary to receive the manifestation.

A.W. Tozer

Stories of Great Young People in the Bible

The great of this world are those who simply loved God more than others did.

A. W. Tozer

The LORD said unto me, Say not, I *am* a child: for thou shalt go to all that I shall send thee, and whatsoever I command thee thou shalt speak.

Jeremiah 1:7

Stories of Great Teens
IN THE BIBLE

Joseph

Joseph was a young man, seventeen years old. . . . Israel made Joseph a special robe with long sleeves. When Joseph's brothers saw that their father loved him more than he loved them, they hated their brother. . . . One time Joseph had a dream, and when he told his brothers about it, they hated him even more. Joseph said, "Listen to the dream I had. We were in the field tying bundles of wheat together. My bundle stood up, and your bundles of wheat gathered around it and bowed down to it." Joseph also told his father about this dream, but his father scolded him, saying, "What kind of dream is this? Do you really believe that your mother, your brothers, and I will bow down to you?" Joseph's brothers were jealous of him, but his father thought about what all these things could mean.

One day . . . Joseph went to look for his brothers and found them in Dothan. . . . Before he reached them, they made a plan to kill him . . . "Let's kill him and throw his body into one of the wells. We can tell our father that a wild animal killed him. Then we will see what will become of his dreams."

Joseph

But Reuben heard their plan and saved Joseph, saying, ". . . Throw him into this well here in the desert, but don't hurt him!" . . . So when Joseph came to his brothers, they pulled off his robe with long sleeves and threw him into the well. . . . When the Midianite traders came by, the brothers took Joseph out of the well and sold him to the Ishmaelites . . . and the Ishmaelites took him to Egypt. The brothers killed a goat and dipped Joseph's robe in its blood. Then they brought the long-sleeved robe to their father and said, "We found this robe. . . ." Jacob looked it over and said, "It is my son's robe! Some savage animal has eaten him. . . . " Then Jacob tore his clothes and put on rough cloth to show that he was upset, and he continued to be sad about his son for a long time.

Meanwhile the Midianites who had bought Joseph had taken him to Egypt. There they sold him to Potiphar, an officer to the king of Egypt and captain of the palace guard.

JOSEPH

Potiphar saw that the Lord was with Joseph and that the Lord made Joseph successful in everything he did. He put Joseph in charge of the house, trusting him with everything he owned. . . . The Lord blessed the people in Potiphar's house because of Joseph. . . .

Now Joseph was well built and handsome. After some time the wife of Joseph's master began to desire Joseph, and . . . the woman talked to Joseph every day, but he refused to have sexual relations with her or even spend time with her. One day . . . his master's wife grabbed his coat and said to him, "Come and have sexual relations with me." But Joseph left his coat in her hand and ran out of the house. . . . She called to the servants in her house and said, "Look! This Hebrew slave was brought here to shame us. He came in and tried to have sexual relations with me. . . . My scream scared him and he ran away, but he left his coat with me." When Joseph's master heard what his wife said Joseph had done, he . . . arrested Joseph and put him into the prison.

Joseph

But the LORD was with Joseph and showed him kindness and caused the prison warden to like Joseph. The prison warden chose Joseph to take care of all the prisoners, and he was responsible for whatever was done in the prison.

Two years later the king dreamed. . . . The next morning the king was troubled about these dreams, . . . but no one could explain their meaning to him. Then the chief officer who served wine to the king said to him, ". . . There was a time when you were angry with the baker and me, and you put us in prison. . . . A young Hebrew man . . . explained their [our dreams'] meanings to us . . . and things happened exactly as he said they would. . . ." So the king called for Joseph . . . The king said to Joseph, ". . . I have heard that you can explain a dream when someone tells it to you." Joseph answered the king, "I am not able to explain the meaning of dreams, but God will do this for the king. . . . Both of these dreams mean the same thing. . . .

JOSEPH

"You will have seven years of good crops. . . . But after those seven years, there will come seven years of hunger. So let the king choose a man who is very wise and understanding and set him over the land of Egypt." So the king said to Joseph, ". . . I will put you in charge of my palace . . . and only I will be greater than you."

And Joseph gathered all the food which was produced in Egypt during those seven years of good crops and stored the food in the cities. . . . Then the seven years of hunger began, just as Joseph had said. . . . And all the people in that part of the world came to Joseph in Egypt to buy grain because the hunger was terrible.

Jacob learned that there was grain in Egypt, so he said to his sons, ". . . Go down there and buy grain for us to eat, so that we will live and not die." So Joseph's brothers came to him and bowed facedown on the ground before him.

JOSEPH

When Joseph saw his brothers, he knew who they were, but he acted as if he didn't know them. . . . And Joseph remembered his dreams about his brothers bowing to him.

When only the brothers were left with Joseph, he told them who he was. "I am your brother Joseph, whom you sold as a slave to go to Egypt. Now don't be worried or angry with yourselves because you sold me here. God sent me here ahead of you . . . to make sure you have some descendants left on earth and to keep you alive in an amazing way. So it was not you who sent me here, but God. God has made me the highest officer of the king of Egypt. I am in charge of his palace, and I am the master of all the land of Egypt."

Genesis 37:2-7,10-12,17-21,24,28,31-34,36; 39:3-7, 10-12,14-15,19-22; 41:1,8-10,12-16,25,29-30,33, 39-40,48,54-57; 42:1-2,6-7,9; 45:1-2,4-5,7-8 NCV

STORIES OF GREAT TEENS IN THE BIBLE

Gideon

The angel of the Lord appeared to Gideon and said, "The Lord is with you, mighty warrior! . . . Go with your strength and save Israel from the Midianites. I am the one who is sending you." But Gideon answered, "Lord, how can I save Israel? My family group is the weakest in Manasseh, and I am the least important member of my family." The Lord answered him, "I will be with you. It will seem as if the Midianites you are fighting are only one man."

The Lord said to Gideon, "You have too many men to defeat the Midianites. I don't want the Israelites to brag that they saved themselves. So now, announce to the people, 'Anyone who is afraid may leave Mount Gilead and go back home.'" So twenty-two thousand men returned home, but ten thousand remained. Then the Lord said to Gideon, "There are still too many men. Take the men down to the water, and I will test them for you there. . . ."

. . . Then the Lord said to Gideon, "Using the three hundred men who lapped the water, I will save you and hand Midian over to you. Let all the others go home."

GIDEON

So Gideon sent the rest of Israel to their homes. . . . That night the LORD said to Gideon, "Get up. Go down and attack the camp of the Midianites, because I will give them to you." So Gideon and his servant Purah went down to the edge of the enemy camp. . . . There were so many of them they seemed like locusts. . . .

Then Gideon went back to the camp of Israel and called out to them, "Get up! The Lord has handed the army of Midian over to you!" Gideon divided the three hundred men into three groups. He gave each man a trumpet and an empty jar with a burning torch inside. Gideon told the men, "Watch me and do what I do. . . . Surround the enemy camp. When I and everyone with me blow our trumpets, you blow your trumpets, too. Then shout, 'For the Lord and for Gideon!'"

So Gideon and the one hundred men with him came to the edge of the enemy camp. . . . Then Gideon and his men blew their trumpets and smashed their jars. All three groups of Gideon's men blew their trumpets and smashed their jars.

GIDEON

They held the torches in their left hands and the trumpets in their right hands. Then they shouted, "A sword for the LORD and for Gideon!" Each of Gideon's men stayed in his place around the camp, but the Midianites began shouting and running to escape. When Gideon's three hundred men blew their trumpets, the Lord made all the Midianites fight each other with their swords! The enemy army ran away.

So Midian was under the rule of Israel; they did not cause trouble anymore. And the land had peace for forty years, as long as Gideon was alive.

Judges 6:12,14-16; 7:2-4,7-9,11-12,15-22; 8:28 NCV

Stories of Great Teens
In the Bible

David

Goliath . . . came out of the Philistine ranks to face the forces of Israel. He was a giant of a man, measuring over nine feet tall! He stood and shouted across to the Israelis, " . . . I will represent the Philistines, and you choose someone to represent you, and we will settle this in single combat! If your man is able to kill me, then we will be your slaves. But if I kill him, then you must be our slaves! I defy the armies of Israel! Send me a man who will fight with me!"

David . . . asked them. "Who is this heathen Philistine, anyway, that he is allowed to defy the armies of the living God?" But when David's oldest brother, Eliab, heard David talking like that, he was angry. "What are you doing around here, anyway? . . . I know what a cocky brat you are; you just want to see the battle!" "What have I done now?" David replied. "I was only asking a question!" . . . When it was finally realized what David meant, someone told King Saul, and the king sent for him.

DAVID

"Don't worry about a thing," David told him. "I'll take care of this Philistine!" "Don't be ridiculous!" Saul replied. "How can a kid like you fight with a man like him? You are only a boy. . . !" But David persisted. " . . . The Lord who saved me from the claws and teeth of the lion and the bear will save me from this Philistine!"

Saul finally consented, "All right, go ahead," he said, "and may the Lord be with you!" Then Saul gave David his own armor. . . . "I can hardly move!" [David] exclaimed, and took them off again. Then he picked up five smooth stones from a stream and put them in his shepherd's bag and, armed only with his shepherd's staff and sling, started across to Goliath. Goliath walked out toward David with his shield-bearer ahead of him, sneering in contempt at this nice little red-cheeked boy!

DAVID

"Am I a dog," he roared at David, "that you come at me with a stick?" And he cursed David by the names of his gods. . . . David shouted in reply, "You come to me with a sword and a spear, but I come to you in the name of the Lord of the armies of heaven and of Israel—the very God whom you have defied. Today the Lord will conquer you and I will kill you and . . . the whole world will know that there is a God in Israel! And Israel will learn that the Lord does not depend on weapons to fulfill his plans—he works without regard to human means! He will give you to us!"

As Goliath approached, David ran out to meet him and, reaching into his shepherd's bag, took out a stone, hurled it from his sling, and hit the Philistine in the forehead. The stone sank in, and the man fell on his face to the ground. So David conquered the Philistine giant with a sling and a stone. . . . Then the Israelis gave a great shout of triumph and rushed after the Philistines . . . and plundered the deserted Philistine camp.

1 Samuel 17:4,8-10,26,28-29,31-34,
37-43,45-50,52-53 TLB

Jonathan

David met Jonathan, the king's son, and there was an immediate bond of love between them. Jonathan swore to be his blood brother, and sealed the pact by giving him his robe, sword, bow, and belt. Saul made [David] commander of his troops. . . . But something had happened . . . after David had killed Goliath. Women came out from all the towns along the way to celebrate and to cheer for King Saul. . . . However, this was their song: "Saul has slain his thousands, and David his ten thousands!" Of course Saul was very angry. . . . So from that time on King Saul kept a jealous watch on David.

Saul now urged his aides and his son Jonathan to assassinate David. But Jonathan, because of his close friendship with David, told him what his father was planning. . . . The next morning as Jonathan and his father were talking together, he spoke well of David and begged him not to be against David. . . . Finally Saul agreed and vowed, "As the Lord lives, he shall not be killed." . . . Then [Jonathan] took David to Saul and everything was as it had been before.

But one day as Saul was sitting at home, listening to David playing the harp, suddenly the tormenting spirit from the Lord attacked him. He had his spear in his hand and hurled it at David in an attempt to kill him. David now fled . . . and found Jonathan. "What have I done?" he exclaimed. "Why is your father so determined to kill me? . . . Your father knows perfectly well about our friendship, so he has said to himself, 'I'll not tell Jonathan. . . .' But the truth is that I am only a step away from death! . . . "

"Tell me what I can do," Jonathan begged.

And David replied, "Tomorrow . . . I'll hide in the field. . . . If your father asks where I am, tell him that I asked permission to go home. . . . If he is angry, then I'll know that he is planning to kill me. Do this for me as my sworn brother."

Jonathan

Jonathan replied . . . "I promise by the Lord God of Israel that . . . I will talk to my father about you and let you know at once how he feels about you. . . . May the Lord be with you as he used to be with my father." . . . So Jonathan made a covenant with the family of David, and David swore to it. . . . But Jonathan made David swear to it again, this time by his love for him, for he loved him as much as he loved himself.

So David hid himself in the field. When . . . the king sat down to eat at his usual place . . . but David's place was empty . . . Saul asked Jonathan, "Why hasn't David been here for dinner either yesterday or today?" "He asked me if he could go to Bethlehem to take part in a family celebration," Jonathan replied. Saul boiled with rage. "You fool!" he yelled at him. "Do you think I don't know that you want this son of a nobody to be king in your place, shaming yourself and your mother? As long as that fellow is alive, you'll never be king. Now go and get him so I can kill him!"

JONATHAN

"But what has he done?" Jonathan demanded. "Why should he be put to death?" Then Saul hurled his spear at Jonathan, intending to kill him; so at last Jonathan realized that his father really meant it when he said David must die. Jonathan left the table in fierce anger and refused to eat all that day, for he was crushed by his father's shameful behavior toward David.

The next morning, as agreed, Jonathan went out into the field. . . . David came out from where he had been hiding. . . . Both of them were crying as they said good-bye, especially David. At last Jonathan said to David, "Cheer up, for we have entrusted each other and each other's children into God's hands forever." So they parted, David going away and Jonathan returning to the city.

David now lived in the wilderness caves. . . . Saul hunted him day after day. . . . (Prince Jonathan now went to find David . . . and encouraged him in his faith in God. "Don't be afraid," Jonathan reassured him. "My father will never find you! You are going to be the king of Israel and I will be next to you, as my father is well aware." So the two of them renewed their pact of friendship. . . .)

JONATHAN

Meanwhile the Philistines had begun the battle against Israel. . . . The Philistines closed in on Saul and killed his son. . . . Jonathan. . . . Saul took his own sword and fell upon the point of the blade. . . . So Saul, his armor bearer, his three sons, and his troops died together that same day.

Then David composed a dirge for Saul and Jonathan. . . .

> O Israel, your pride and joy lies dead upon the hills;
> Mighty heroes have fallen. . . .
> How I weep for you, my brother Jonathan;
> How much I loved you!
> And your love for me was deeper
> Than the love of women!

1 Samuel 18:1-9; 19:1-2,4,6-7,9-10;
20:1,3-8,11-13,16-17,24-25,27-35,41-42;
23:14-18; 31:1-2,4,6;
2 Samuel 1:17-19,26 TLB

IN THE BIBLE

Daniel, Shadrach, Meshach, Abednego

King Nebuchadnezzar . . . ordered Ashpenaz, who was in charge of the palace officials, to bring to the palace some of the young men of Judah's royal family and other noble families, who had been brought to Babylon as captives. "Select only strong, healthy, and good-looking young men," he said. "Make sure they are well versed in every branch of learning, are gifted with knowledge and good sense, and have the poise needed to serve in the royal palace. Teach these young men the language and literature of the Babylonians." The king assigned them a daily ration of the best food and wine from his own kitchens. They were to be trained for a three-year period, and then some of them would be made his advisers in the royal court. Daniel, Hananiah, Mishael, and Azariah were four of the young men chosen, all from the tribe of Judah. The chief official renamed them with these Babylonian names:

Daniel was called Belteshazzar.
Hananiah was called Shadrach.
Mishael was called Meshach.
Azariah was called Abednego.

But Daniel made up his mind not to defile himself by eating the food and wine given to them by the king. "Test us for ten days on a diet of vegetables and water," Daniel said.

DANIEL, SHADRACH, MESHACH, ABEDNEGO

"At the end of the ten days, see how we look compared to the other young men who are eating the king's rich food. Then you can decide whether or not to let us continue eating our diet." So the attendant agreed to Daniel's suggestion and tested them for ten days.

At the end of the ten days, Daniel and his three friends looked healthier and better nourished than the young men who had been eating the food assigned by the king. So after that, the attendant fed them only vegetables instead of the rich foods and wines. God gave these four young men an unusual aptitude for learning the literature and science of the time. And God gave Daniel special ability in understanding the meanings of visions and dreams.

When the three-year training period ordered by the king was completed, the chief official brought all the young men to King Nebuchadnezzar. The king talked with each of them, and none of them impressed him as much as Daniel, Hananiah, Mishael, and Azariah. So they were appointed to his regular staff of advisers. In all matters requiring wisdom and balanced judgment, the king found the advice of these young men to be ten times better than that of all the magicians and enchanters in his entire kingdom.

Daniel 1:1,3-8,12-20 NLT

Daniel

[King] Nebuchadnezzar . . . called in his magicians, enchanters, sorcerers, and astrologers, and he demanded . . . , "I have had a dream that troubles me. Tell me what I dreamed, for I must know what it means." . . . The astrologers replied to the king, "There isn't a man alive who can tell Your Majesty his dream! . . . No one except the gods can tell you your dream, and they do not live among people."

The king was furious when he heard this, and he sent out orders to execute all the wise men of Babylon. . . . Then Daniel went home and told his friends. . . . He urged them to ask the God of heaven to show them his mercy by telling them the secret, so they would not be executed along with the other wise men of Babylon. That night the secret was revealed to Daniel in a vision.

Then Arioch quickly took Daniel to the king and said, "I have found one of the captives from Judah who will tell Your Majesty the meaning of your dream!" The king said to Daniel . . . , "Is this true? Can you tell me what my dream was and what it means?"

Daniel

Daniel replied, ". . . There is a God in heaven who reveals secrets, and he has shown King Nebuchadnezzar what will happen in the future. . . . It is not because I am wiser than any living person that I know the secret of your dream, but because God wanted you to understand what you were thinking about.

"Your Majesty, in your vision you saw in front of you a huge and powerful statue. . . . The head of the statue was made of fine gold, its chest and arms were of silver, its belly and thighs were of bronze, its legs were of iron, and its feet were a combination of iron and clay. But as you watched, a rock was cut from a mountain by supernatural means. It struck the feet of iron and clay, smashing them to bits. . . . The pieces were crushed as small as chaff on a threshing floor, and the wind blew them all away without a trace. But the rock that knocked the statue down became a great mountain that covered the whole earth.

"That was the dream; now I will tell Your Majesty what it means. . . . The God of heaven . . . has made you the ruler over all the inhabited world and has put even the animals and birds under your control. You are the head of gold.

"But after your kingdom comes to an end, another great kingdom, inferior to yours, will rise to take your place. After that kingdom has fallen, yet a third great kingdom, represented by the bronze belly and thighs, will rise to rule the world. Following that kingdom, there will be a fourth great kingdom, as strong as iron. That kingdom will smash and crush all previous empires, just as iron smashes and crushes everything it strikes. The feet and toes you saw that were a combination of iron and clay show that this kingdom will be divided. Some parts of it will be as strong as iron, and others as weak as clay. This mixture of iron and clay also shows that these kingdoms will try to strengthen themselves by forming alliances with each other through intermarriage. But this will not succeed, just as iron and clay do not mix.

Daniel

"During the reigns of those kings, the God of heaven will set up a kingdom that will never be destroyed; no one will ever conquer it. It will shatter all these kingdoms into nothingness, but it will stand forever. That is the meaning of the rock cut from the mountain by supernatural means, crushing to dust the statue of iron, bronze, clay, silver, and gold. . . ."

The king said to Daniel, "Truly, your God is the God of gods, the Lord over kings, a revealer of mysteries, for you have been able to reveal this secret." Then the king appointed Daniel to a high position and gave him many valuable gifts. He made Daniel ruler over the whole province of Babylon, as well as chief over all his wise men.

Daniel 2:1-3,10-12,17-19,25-28,30-45,47-48 NLT

Shadrach, Meshach, and Abednego

King Nebuchadnezzar made a gold statue . . . and set it up . . . in the province of Babylon. . . . When all these officials had arrived and were standing before the image King Nebuchadnezzar had set up, a herald shouted out, "People of all races and nations and languages, listen to the king's command! When you hear the sound of the horn, flute, zither, lyre, harp, pipes, and other instruments, bow to the ground to worship King Nebuchadnezzar's gold statue. Anyone who refuses to obey will immediately be thrown into a blazing furnace." So at the sound of the musical instruments, all the people, whatever their race or nation or language, bowed to the ground and worshiped the statue that King Nebuchadnezzar had set up.

But some of the astrologers went to the king and informed on the Jews. They said to King Nebuchadnezzar, "Long live the king! You issued a decree requiring all the people to bow down and worship the gold statue when they hear the sound of the musical instruments. That decree also states that those who refuse to obey must be thrown into a blazing furnace. But there are some Jews—Shadrach, Meshach, and Abednego—whom you have put in charge of the province of Babylon. They have defied Your Majesty by refusing to serve your gods or to worship the gold statue you have set up."

Then Nebuchadnezzar flew into a rage and ordered Shadrach, Meshach, and Abednego to be brought before him. When they were brought in, Nebuchadnezzar said to them, "Is it true, Shadrach, Meshach, and Abednego, that you refuse to serve my gods or to worship the gold statue I have set up? . . ." Shadrach, Meshach, and Abednego replied, "O Nebuchadnezzar, we do not need to defend ourselves before you. If we are thrown into the blazing furnace, the God whom we serve is able to save us. He will rescue us from your power, Your Majesty. But even if he doesn't, Your Majesty can be sure that we will never serve your gods or worship the gold statue you have set up."

Nebuchadnezzar was so furious . . . he . . . commanded that the furnace be heated seven times hotter than usual. Then he ordered some of the strongest men of his army to bind Shadrach, Meshach, and Abednego and throw them into the blazing furnace. . . . The flames leaped out and killed the soldiers as they threw the three men in!

. . . As he was watching, Nebuchadnezzar jumped up in amazement and exclaimed to his advisers, "Didn't we tie up three men and throw them into the furnace?"

SHADRACH, MESHACH, AND ABEDNEGO

"Yes," they said, "we did indeed, Your Majesty." "Look!" Nebuchadnezzar shouted. "I see four men, unbound, walking around in the fire. They aren't even hurt by the flames! And the fourth looks like a divine being! . . . Shadrach, Meshach, and Abednego, servants of the Most High God, come out! Come here!" So Shadrach, Meshach, and Abednego stepped out of the fire. . . . Not a hair on their heads was singed, and their clothing was not scorched. They didn't even smell of smoke!

Then Nebuchadnezzar said, "Praise to the God of Shadrach, Meshach, and Abednego! He sent his angel to rescue his servants who trusted in him. They defied the king's command and were willing to die rather than serve or worship any god except their own God. Therefore, I make this decree: If any people, whatever their race or nation or language, speak a word against the God of Shadrach, Meshach, and Abednego, they will be torn limb from limb, and their houses will be crushed into heaps of rubble. There is no other god who can rescue like this!" Then the king promoted Shadrach, Meshach, and Abednego to even higher positions in the province of Babylon.

Daniel 3:1,3-14,16-20,22,24-30 NLT

PRAYERS BY GREAT YOUNG PEOPLE IN THE BIBLE

Prayer is an invisible tool which
is wielded in a visible world.

Ed Cole

Pray in the Spirit at all times with all kinds of prayers, asking for everything you need. To do this you must always be ready and never give up. Always pray for all God's people.

Ephesians 6:18 NCV

Prayers by Great Young People
IN THE BIBLE

Solomon

At Gibeon the LORD appeared to Solomon during the night in a dream, and God said, "Ask for whatever you want me to give you."

Solomon answered, "You have shown great kindness to your servant, my father David, because he was faithful to you and righteous and upright in heart. . . .

"Now, O LORD my God, you have made your servant king in place of my father David. But I am only a little child and do not know how to carry out my duties. Your servant is here among the people you have chosen, a great people, too numerous to count or number. So give your servant a discerning heart to govern your people and to distinguish between right and wrong. For who is able to govern this great people of yours?"

The Lord was pleased that Solomon had asked for this. So God said to him, "Since you have asked for this and not for long life or wealth for yourself, nor have asked for the death of your enemies but for discernment in administering justice, I will do what you have asked. I will give you a wise and discerning heart, so that there will never have been anyone like you, nor will there ever be. Moreover, I will give you what you have not asked for—both riches and honor—so that in your lifetime you will have no equal among kings. And if you walk in my ways and obey my statutes and commands as David your father did, I will give you a long life."

1 Kings 3:5-15 NIV

David

THE LORD *is* my shepherd;
I shall not want.
He makes me to lie down in green pastures;
He leads me beside the still waters.
He restores my soul;
He leads me in the paths of righteousness
For His name's sake.
Yea, though I walk through the valley of the
shadow of death,
I will fear no evil;
For You *are* with me;
Your rod and Your staff, they comfort me.
You prepare a table before me in the presence of
my enemies;
You anoint my head with oil;
My cup runs over.
Surely goodness and mercy shall follow me
All the days of my life;
And I will dwell in the house of the LORD
Forever.

Psalm 23 NKJV

PRAYERS BY GREAT YOUNG PEOPLE
IN THE BIBLE

Daniel

"Praise the name of God forever and ever,
for he alone has all wisdom and power.
He determines the course of world events;
he removes kings and sets others on the throne.
He gives wisdom to the wise
and knowledge to the scholars.
He reveals deep and mysterious things
and knows what lies hidden in darkness,
though he himself is surrounded by light.
I thank and praise you, God of my ancestors,
for you have given me wisdom and strength.
You have told me what we asked of you
and revealed to us what the king demanded."

Daniel 2:20-23 NLT

PRAYERS BY GREAT YOUNG PEOPLE IN THE BIBLE

Mary

Mary said [to Elizabeth],
"I'm bursting with God-news;
I'm dancing the song of my Savior God.
God took one good look at me, and look
    what happened—
I'm the most fortunate woman on earth!
What God has done for me will never be forgotten,
the God whose very name is holy, set apart from
    all others.
His mercy flows in wave after wave
on those who are in awe before him.
He bared his arm and showed his strength,
scattered the bluffing braggarts.
He knocked tyrants off their high horses,
pulled victims out of the mud.
The starving poor sat down to a banquet;
the callous rich were left out in the cold.
He embraced his chosen child, Israel;
he remembered and piled on the mercies, piled
    them high.
It's exactly what he promised,
beginning with Abraham and right up to now."

Luke 1:46-55 THE MESSAGE

GOD SPEAKS TO TEENS

Young people do the impossible
before they find out it's impossible—
that's why God uses them so often.
Loren Cunningham

Jesus came and told his disciples, "I have been given complete authority in heaven and on earth. Therefore, go and make disciples of all the nations, baptizing them in the name of the Father and the Son and the Holy Spirit. Teach these new disciples to obey all the commands I have given you. And be sure of this: I am with you always, even to the end of the age."

Matthew 28: 18-20 NLT

GOD SPEAKS TO TEENS

David to Solomon
Do Not Let Sinners Entice You

Listen, my son, to your father's instruction
and do not forsake your mother's teaching.
They will be a garland to grace your head
and a chain to adorn your neck.
My son, if sinners entice you,
do not give in to them.
If they say, "Come along with us;
let's lie in wait for someone's blood,
let's waylay some harmless soul;
let's swallow them alive, like the grave,
and whole, like those who go down to the pit;
we will get all sorts of valuable things
and fill our houses with plunder;
throw in your lot with us,
and we will share a common purse"—
my son, do not go along with them,
do not set foot on their paths;
for their feet rush into sin,
they are swift to shed blood.

Proverbs 1:8-16 NIV

Treasure Wisdom

My son, if you accept my words and store up my commands within you,
turning your ear to wisdom
and applying your heart to understanding,
and if you call out for insight
and cry aloud for understanding,
and if you look for it as for silver
and search for it as for hidden treasure,
then you will understand the fear of the LORD
and find the knowledge of God.

Proverbs 2:1-5 NIV

Trust in the Lord

My son, do not forget my teaching,
but keep my commands in your heart,
for they will prolong your life many years
and bring you prosperity.
Let love and faithfulness never leave you;
bind them around your neck,
write them on the tablet of your heart.
Then you will win favor and a good name
in the sight of God and man.
Trust in the LORD with all your heart
and lean not on your own understanding;

in all your ways acknowledge him,
and he will make your paths straight.
Do not be wise in your own eyes;
fear the LORD and shun evil.
This will bring health to your body
and nourishment to your bones.
Honor the LORD with your wealth,
with the firstfruits of all your crops;
then your barns will be filled to overflowing,
and your vats will brim over with new wine.
My son, do not despise the LORD's discipline
and do not resent his rebuke,
because the LORD disciplines those he loves,
as a father the son he delights in.

Proverbs 3:1-12 NIV

Beware of Flattering Speech

I . . . saw a simple-minded . . . young man who lacked common sense. He was crossing the street near the house of an immoral woman . . . The woman approached him, dressed seductively and sly of heart . . .

So she seduced him with her pretty speech. With her flattery she enticed him. He followed her at once, like an ox going to the slaughter or like a trapped stag, awaiting the arrow that would pierce its heart. He was like a bird flying into a snare, little knowing it would cost him his life . . .

Don't wander down her wayward path. For she has been the ruin of many; numerous men have been her victims. Her house is the road to the grave. Her bedroom is the den of death.

Proverbs 7:6-27 TLB

Bathsheba to Solomon
Help Those in Need

What, O my son?
And what, O son of my womb?
And what, O son of my vows?
Do not give your strength to women,
Or your ways to that which destroys kings.
It is not for kings, O Lemuel,
It is not for kings to drink wine,
Or for rulers to desire strong drink,
For they will drink and forget what is decreed,
And pervert the rights of all the afflicted . . .
Open your mouth for the mute,
For the rights of all the unfortunate.
Open your mouth, judge righteously,
And defend the rights of the afflicted and needy.

Proverbs 31:2-5,8-9 NASB

The Lord to Jeremiah
You Are Not Too Young!

The Lord said to [Jeremiah], "I knew you before you were formed within your mother's womb; before you were born I sanctified you and appointed you as my spokesman to the world."

"O Lord God," I said, "I can't do that! I'm far too young! I'm only a youth!"

"Don't say that," he replied, "for you will go wherever I send you and speak whatever I tell you to. And don't be afraid of the people, for I, the Lord, will be with you and see you through."

Then he touched my mouth and said, "See, I have put my words in your mouth!"

Jeremiah 1:4-9 TLB

Paul to Timothy
Don't Let Anyone Tell You That You Are Too Young

Let no one despise your youth, but be an example to the believers in word, in conduct, in love, in spirit, in faith, in purity. Till I come, give attention to reading, to exhortation, to doctrine. Do not neglect the gift that is in you, which was given to you by prophecy with the laying on of the hands of the eldership. Meditate on these things; give yourself entirely to them, that your progress may be evident to all. Take heed to yourself and to the doctrine. Continue in them, for in doing this you will save both yourself and those who hear you.

1 Timothy 4:12-16 NKJV

THROUGH THE BIBLE IN ONE YEAR

A knowledge of the Bible without a college course is more valuable than a college course without the Bible.

Williams Lyon Phelps

There's nothing like the written Word of God for showing you the way to salvation through faith in Christ Jesus. Every part of Scripture is God-breathed and useful one way or another—showing us truth, exposing our rebellion, correcting our mistakes, training us to live God's way. Through the Word we are put together and shaped up for the tasks God has for us.

2 Timothy 3:15-17 THE MESSAGE

THROUGH THE BIBLE IN ONE YEAR

January

1. Genesis 1-2; Psalm 1; Matthew 1-2
2. Genesis 3-4; Psalm 2; Matthew 3-4
3. Genesis 5-7; Psalm 3; Matthew 5
4. Genesis 8-9; Psalm 4; Matthew 6-7
5. Genesis 10-11; Psalm 5; Matthew 8-9
6. Genesis 12-13; Psalm 6; Matthew 10-11
7. Genesis 14-15; Psalm 7; Matthew 12
8. Genesis 16-17; Psalm 8; Matthew 13
9. Genesis 18-19; Psalm 9; Matthew 14-15
10. Genesis 20-21; Psalm 10; Matthew 16-17
11. Genesis 22-23; Psalm 11; Matthew 18
12. Genesis 24; Psalm 12; Matthew 19-20
13. Genesis 25-26; Psalm 13; Matthew 21
14. Genesis 27-28; Psalm 14; Matthew 22
15. Genesis 29-30; Psalm 15; Matthew 23
16. Genesis 31-32; Psalm 16; Matthew 24
17. Genesis 33-34; Psalm 17; Matthew 25
18. Genesis 35-36; Psalm 18; Matthew 26
19. Genesis 37-38; Psalm 19; Matthew 27
20. Genesis 39-40; Psalm 20; Matthew 28
21. Genesis 41-42; Psalm 21; Mark 1
22. Genesis 43-44; Psalm 22; Mark 2
23. Genesis 45-46; Psalm 23; Mark 3
24. Genesis 47-48; Psalm 24; Mark 4
25. Genesis 49-50; Psalm 25; Mark 5
26. Exodus 1-2; Psalm 26; Mark 6
27. Exodus 3-4; Psalm 27; Mark 7
28. Exodus 5-6; Psalm 28; Mark 8
29. Exodus 7-8; Psalm 29; Mark 9
30. Exodus 9-10; Psalm 30; Mark 10
31. Exodus 11-12; Psalm 31; Mark 11

Through the Bible in One Year

February

1. Exodus 13-14; Psalm 32; Mark 12
2. Exodus 15-16; Psalm 33; Mark 13
3. Exodus 17-18; Psalm 34; Mark 14
4. Exodus 19-20; Psalm 35; Mark 15
5. Exodus 21-22; Psalm 36; Mark 16
6. Exodus 23-24; Psalm 37; Luke 1
7. Exodus 25-26; Psalm 38; Luke 2
8. Exodus 27-28; Psalm 39; Luke 3
9. Exodus 29-30; Psalm 40; Luke 4
10. Exodus 31-32; Psalm 41; Luke 5
11. Exodus 33-34; Psalm 42; Luke 6
12. Exodus 35-36; Psalm 43; Luke 7
13. Exodus 37-38; Psalm 44; Luke 8
14. Exodus 39-40; Psalm 45; Luke 9
15. Leviticus 1-2; Psalm 46; Luke 10
16. Leviticus 3-4; Psalm 47; Luke 11
17. Leviticus 5-6; Psalm 48; Luke 12
18. Leviticus 7-8; Psalm 49; Luke 13
19. Leviticus 9-10; Psalm 50; Luke 14
20. Leviticus 11-12; Psalm 51; Luke 15
21. Leviticus 13; Psalm 52; Luke 16
22. Leviticus 14; Psalm 53; Luke 17
23. Leviticus 15-16; Psalm 54; Luke 18
24. Leviticus 17-18; Psalm 55; Luke 19
25. Leviticus 19-20; Psalm 56; Luke 20
26. Leviticus 21-22; Psalm 57; Luke 21
27. Leviticus 23-24; Psalm 58; Luke 22
28. Leviticus 25; Psalm 59; Luke 23

Through the Bible

in One Year

March

1. Leviticus 26-27; Psalm 60; Luke 24
2. Numbers 1-2; Psalm 61; John 1
3. Numbers 3-4; Psalm 62; John 2-3
4. Numbers 5-6; Psalm 63; John 4
5. Numbers 7; Psalm 64; John 5
6. Numbers 8-9; Psalm 65; John 6
7. Numbers 10-11; Psalm 66; John 7
8. Numbers 12-13; Psalm 67; John 8
9. Numbers 14-15; Psalm 68; John 9
10. Numbers 16; Psalm 69; John 10
11. Numbers 17-18; Psalm 70; John 11
12. Numbers 19-20; Psalm 71; John 12
13. Numbers 21-22; Psalm 72; John 13
14. Numbers 23-24; Psalm 73; John 14-15
15. Numbers 25-26; Psalm 74; John 16
16. Numbers 27-28; Psalm 75; John 17
17. Numbers 29-30; Psalm 76; John 18
18. Numbers 31-32; Psalm 77; John 19
19. Numbers 33-34; Psalm 78; John 20
20. Numbers 35-36; Psalm 79; John 21
21. Deuteronomy 1-2; Psalm 80; Acts 1
22. Deuteronomy 3-4; Psalm 81; Acts 2
23. Deuteronomy 5-6; Psalm 82; Acts 3-4
24. Deuteronomy 7-8; Psalm 83; Acts 5-6
25. Deuteronomy 9-10; Psalm 84; Acts 7
26. Deuteronomy 11-12; Psalm 85; Acts 8
27. Deuteronomy 13-14; Psalm 86; Acts 9
28. Deuteronomy 15-16; Psalm 87; Acts 10
29. Deuteronomy 17-18; Psalm 88; Acts 11-12
30. Deuteronomy 19-20; Psalm 89; Acts 13
31. Deuteronomy 21-22; Psalm 90; Acts 14

Through the Bible in One Year

April

1. Deuteronomy 23-24; Psalm 91; Acts 15
2. Deuteronomy 25-27; Psalm 92; Acts 16
3. Deuteronomy 28-29; Psalm 93; Acts 17
4. Deuteronomy 30-31; Psalm 94; Acts 18
5. Deuteronomy 32; Psalm 95; Acts 19
6. Deuteronomy 33-34; Psalm 96; Acts 20
7. Joshua 1-2; Psalm 97; Acts 21
8. Joshua 3-4; Psalm 98; Acts 22
9. Joshua 5-6; Psalm 99; Acts 23
10. Joshua 7-8; Psalm 100; Acts 24-25
11. Joshua 9-10; Psalm 101; Acts 26
12. Joshua 11-12; Psalm 102; Acts 27
13. Joshua 13-14; Psalm 103; Acts 28
14. Joshua 15-16; Psalm 104; Romans 1-2
15. Joshua 17-18; Psalm 105; Romans 3-4
16. Joshua 19-20; Psalm 106; Romans 5-6
17. Joshua 21-22; Psalm 107; Romans 7-8
18. Joshua 23-24; Psalm 108; Romans 9-10
19. Judges 1-2; Psalm 109; Romans 11-12
20. Judges 3-4; Psalm 110; Romans 13-14
21. Judges 5-6; Psalm 111; Romans 15-16
22. Judges 7-8; Psalm 112; 1 Corinthians 1-2
23. Judges 9; Psalm 113; 1 Corinthians 3-4
24. Judges 10-11; Psalm 114; 1 Corinthians 5-6
25. Judges 12-13; Psalm 115; 1 Corinthians 7
26. Judges 14-15; Psalm 116; 1 Corinthians 8-9
27. Judges 16-17; Psalm 117; 1 Corinthians 10
28. Judges 18-19; Psalm 118; 1 Corinthians 11
29. Judges 20-21; Psalm 119:1-88; 1 Corinthians 12
30. Ruth 1-4; Psalm 119:89-176; 1 Corinthians 13

Through the Bible in One Year

May

1. 1 Samuel 1-2; Psalm 120; 1 Corinthians 14
2. 1 Samuel 3-4; Psalm 121; 1 Corinthians 15
3. 1 Samuel 5-6; Psalm 122; 1 Corinthians 16
4. 1 Samuel 7-8; Psalm 123; 2 Corinthians 1
5. 1 Samuel 9-10; Psalm 124; 2 Corinthians 2-3
6. 1 Samuel 11-12; Psalm 125; 2 Corinthians 4-5
7. 1 Samuel 13-14; Psalm 126; 2 Corinthians 6-7
8. 1 Samuel 15-16; Psalm 127; 2 Corinthians 8
9. 1 Samuel 17; Psalm 128; 2 Corinthians 9-10
10. 1 Samuel 18-19; Psalm 129; 2 Corinthians 11
11. 1 Samuel 20-21; Psalm 130; 2 Corinthians 12
12. 1 Samuel 22-23; Psalm 131; 2 Corinthians 13
13. 1 Samuel 24-25; Psalm 132; Galatians 1-2
14. 1 Samuel 26-27; Psalm 133; Galatians 3-4
15. 1 Samuel 28-29; Psalm 134; Galatians 5-6
16. 1 Samuel 30-31; Psalm 135; Ephesians 1-2
17. 2 Samuel 1-2; Psalm 136; Ephesians 3-4
18. 2 Samuel 3-4; Psalm 137; Ephesians 5-6
19. 2 Samuel 5-6; Psalm 138; Philippians 1-2
20. 2 Samuel 7-8; Psalm 139; Philippians 3-4
21. 2 Samuel 9-10; Psalm 140; Colossians 1-2
22. 2 Samuel 11-12; Psalm 141; Colossians 3-4
23. 2 Samuel 13-14; Psalm 142; 1 Thessalonians 1-2
24. 2 Samuel 15-16; Psalm 143; 1 Thessalonians 3-4
25. 2 Samuel 17-18; Psalm 144; 1 Thessalonians 5
26. 2 Samuel 19; Psalm 145; 2 Thessalonians 1-3
27. 2 Samuel 20-21; Psalm 146; 1 Timothy 1-2
28. 2 Samuel 22; Psalm 147; 1 Timothy 3-4
29. 2 Samuel 23-24; Psalm 148; 1 Timothy 5-6
30. 1 Kings 1; Psalm 149; 2 Timothy 1-2
31. 1 Kings 2-3; Psalm 150; 2 Timothy 3-4

Through the Bible
in One Year

June

1. 1 Kings 4-5; Proverbs 1; Titus 1-3
2. 1 Kings 6-7; Proverbs 2; Philemon
3. 1 Kings 8; Proverbs 3; Hebrew 1-2
4. 1 Kings 9-10; Proverbs 4; Hebrew 3-4
5. 1 Kings 11-12; Proverbs 5; Hebrews 5-6
6. 1 Kings 13-14; Proverbs 6; Hebrews 7-8
7. 1 Kings 15-16; Proverbs 7; Hebrews 9-10
8. 1 Kings 17-18; Proverbs 8; Hebrews 11
9. 1 Kings 19-20; Proverbs 9; Hebrews 12
10. 1 Kings 21-22; Proverbs 10; Hebrews 13
11. 2 Kings 1-2; Proverbs 11; James 1
12. 2 Kings 3-4; Proverbs 12; James 2-3
13. 2 Kings 5-6; Proverbs 13; James 4-5
14. 2 Kings 7-8; Proverbs 14; 1 Peter 1
15. 2 Kings 9-10; Proverbs 15; 1 Peter 2-3
16. 2 Kings 11-12; Proverbs 16; 1 Peter 4-5
17. 2 Kings 13-14; Proverbs 17; 2 Peter 1-3
18. 2 Kings 15-16; Proverbs 18; 1 John 1-2
19. 2 Kings 17; Proverbs 19; 1 John 3-4
20. 2 Kings 18-19; Proverbs 20; 1 John 5
21. 2 Kings 20-21; Proverbs 21; 2 John
22. 2 Kings 22-23; Proverbs 22; 3 John
23. 2 Kings 24-25; Proverbs 23; Jude
24. 1 Chronicles 1; Proverbs 24; Revelation 1-2
25. 1 Chronicles 2-3; Proverbs 25; Revelation 3-5
26. 1 Chronicles 4-5; Proverbs 26; Revelation 6-7
27. 1 Chronicles 6-7; Proverbs 27; Revelation 8-10
28. 1 Chronicles 8-9; Proverbs 28; Revelation 11-12
29. 1 Chronicles 10-11; Proverbs 29; Revelation 13-14
30. 1 Chronicles 12-13; Proverbs 30, Revelation 15-17

Through the Bible
in One Year

July

1. 1 Chronicles 14-15; Proverbs 31; Revelation 18-19
2. 1 Chronicles 16-17; Psalm 1; Revelation 20-22
3. 1 Chronicles 18-19; Psalm 2; Matthew 1-2
4. 1 Chronicles 20-21; Psalm 3; Matthew 3-4
5. 1 Chronicles 22-23; Psalm 4; Matthew 5
6. 1 Chronicles 24-25; Psalm 5; Matthew 6-7
7. 1 Chronicles 26-27; Psalm 6; Matthew 8-9
8. 1 Chronicles 28-29; Psalm 7; Matthew 10-11
9. 2 Chronicles 1-2; Psalm 8; Matthew 12
10. 2 Chronicles 3-4; Psalm 9; Matthew 13
11. 2 Chronicles 5-6; Psalm 10; Matthew 14-15
12. 2 Chronicles 7-8; Psalm 11; Matthew 16-17
13. 2 Chronicles 9-10; Psalm 12; Matthew 18
14. 2 Chronicles 11-12; Psalm 13; Matthew 19-20
15. 2 Chronicles 13-14; Psalm 14; Matthew 21
16. 2 Chronicles 15-16; Psalm 15; Matthew 22
17. 2 Chronicles 17-18; Psalm 16; Matthew 23
18. 2 Chronicles 19-20; Psalm 17; Matthew 24
19. 2 Chronicles 21-22; Psalm 18; Matthew 25
20. 2 Chronicles 23-24; Psalm 19; Matthew 26
21. 2 Chronicles 25-26; Psalm 20; Matthew 27
22. 2 Chronicles 27-28; Psalm 21; Matthew 28
23. 2 Chronicles 29-30; Psalm 22; Mark 1
24. 2 Chronicles 31-32; Psalm 23; Mark 2
25. 2 Chronicles 33-34; Psalm 24; Mark 3
26. 2 Chronicles 35-36; Psalm 25; Mark 4
27. Ezra 1-2; Psalm 26; Mark 5
28. Ezra 3-4; Psalm 27; Mark 6
29. Ezra 5-6; Psalm 28; Mark 7
30. Ezra 7-8; Psalm 29; Mark 8
31. Ezra 9-10; Psalm 30; Mark 9

Through the Bible in One Year

August

1. Nehemiah 1-2; Psalm 31; Mark 10
2. Nehemiah 3-4; Psalm 32; Mark 11
3. Nehemiah 5-6; Psalm 33; Mark 12
4. Nehemiah 7; Psalm 34; Mark 13
5. Nehemiah 8-9; Psalm 35; Mark 14
6. Nehemiah 10-11; Psalm 36; Mark 15
7. Nehemiah 12-13; Psalm 37; Mark 16
8. Esther 1-2; Psalm 38; Luke 1
9. Esther 3-4; Psalm 39; Luke 2
10. Esther 5-6; Psalm 40; Luke 3
11. Esther 7-8; Psalm 41; Luke 4
12. Esther 9-10; Psalm 42; Luke 5
13. Job 1-2; Psalm 43; Luke 6
14. Job 3-4; Psalm 44; Luke 7
15. Job 5-6; Psalm 45; Luke 8
16. Job 7-8; Psalm 46; Luke 9
17. Job 9-10; Psalm 47; Luke 10
18. Job 11-12; Psalm 48; Luke 11
19. Job 13-14; Psalm 49; Luke 12
20. Job 15-16; Psalm 50; Luke 13
21. Job 17-18; Psalm 51; Luke 14
22. Job 19-20; Psalm 52; Luke 15
23. Job 21-22; Psalm 53; Luke 16
24. Job 23-25; Psalm 54; Luke 17
25. Job 26-28; Psalm 55; Luke 18
26. Job 29-30; Psalm 56; Luke 19
27. Job 31-32; Psalm 57; Luke 20
28. Job 33-34; Psalm 58; Luke 21
29. Job 35-36; Psalm 59; Luke 22
30. Job 37-38; Psalm 60; Luke 23
31. Job 39-40; Psalm 61; Luke 24

in One Year

September

1. Job 41-42; Psalm 62; John 1
2. Ecclesiastes 1-2; Psalm 63; John 2-3
3. Ecclesiastes 3-4; Psalm 64; John 4
4. Ecclesiastes 5-6; Psalm 65; John 5
5. Ecclesiastes 7-8; Psalm 66; John 6
6. Ecclesiastes 9-10; Psalm 67; John 7
7. Ecclesiastes 11-12; Psalm 68; John 8
8. Song of Solomon 1-2; Psalm 69; John 9
9. Song of Solomon 3-4; Psalm 70; John 10
10. Song of Solomon 5-6; Psalm 71; John 11
11. Song of Solomon 7-8; Psalm 72; John 12
12. Isaiah 1-2; Psalm 73; John 13
13. Isaiah 3-5; Psalm 74; John 14-15
14. Isaiah 6-8; Psalm 75; John 16
15. Isaiah 9-10; Psalm 76; John 17
16. Isaiah 11-13; Psalm 77; John 18
17. Isaiah 14-15; Psalm 78; John 19
18. Isaiah 16-17; Psalm 79; John 20
19. Isaiah 18-19; Psalm 80; John 21
20. Isaiah 20-22; Psalm 81; Acts 1
21. Isaiah 23-24; Psalm 82; Acts 2
22. Isaiah 25-26; Psalm 83; Acts 3-4
23. Isaiah 27-28; Psalm 84; Acts 5-6
24. Isaiah 29-30; Psalm 85; Acts 7
25. Isaiah 31-32; Psalm 86; Acts 8
26. Isaiah 33-34; Psalm 87; Acts 9
27. Isaiah 35-36; Psalm 88; Acts 10
28. Isaiah 37-38; Psalm 89; Acts 11-12
29. Isaiah 39-40; Psalm 90; Acts 13
30. Isaiah 41-42; Psalm 91; Acts 14

Through the Bible in One Year

October

1. Isaiah 43-44; Psalm 92; Acts 15
2. Isaiah 45-46; Psalm 93; Acts 16
3. Isaiah 47-48; Psalm 94; Acts 17
4. Isaiah 49-50; Psalm 95; Acts 18
5. Isaiah 51-52; Psalm 96; Acts 19
6. Isaiah 53-54; Psalm 97; Acts 20
7. Isaiah 55-56; Psalm 98; Acts 21
8. Isaiah 57-58; Psalm 99; Acts 22
9. Isaiah 59-60; Psalm 100; Acts 23
10. Isaiah 61-62; Psalm 101; Acts 24-25
11. Isaiah 63-64; Psalm 102; Acts 26
12. Isaiah 65-66; Psalm 103; Acts 27
13. Jeremiah 1-2; Psalm 104; Acts 28
14. Jeremiah 3-4; Psalm 105; Romans 1-2
15. Jeremiah 5-6; Psalm 106; Romans 3-4
16. Jeremiah 7-8; Psalm 107; Romans 5-6
17. Jeremiah 9-10; Psalm 108; Romans 7-8
18. Jeremiah 11-12; Psalm 109; Romans 9-10
19. Jeremiah 13-14; Psalm 110; Romans 11-12
20. Jeremiah 15-16; Psalm 111; Romans 13-14
21. Jeremiah 17-18; Psalm 112; Romans 15-16
22. Jeremiah 19-20; Psalm 113; 1 Corinthians 1-2
23. Jeremiah 21-22; Psalm 114; 1 Corinthians 3-4
24. Jeremiah 23-24; Psalm 115; 1 Corinthians 5-6
25. Jeremiah 25-26; Psalm 116; 1 Corinthians 7
26. Jeremiah 27-28; Psalm 117; 1 Corinthians 8-9
27. Jeremiah 29-30; Psalm 118; 1 Corinthians 10
28. Jeremiah 31-32; Psalm 119: 1-64; 1 Corinthians 11
29. Jeremiah 33-34; Psalm 119:65-120; 1 Corinthians 12
30. Jeremiah 35-36; Psalm 119:121-176; 1 Corinthians 13
31. Jeremiah 37-38; Psalm 120; 1 Corinthians 14

Through the Bible in One Year

November

1. Jeremiah 39-40; Psalm 121; 1 Corinthians 15
2. Jeremiah 41-42; Psalm 122; 1 Corinthians 16
3. Jeremiah 43-44; Psalm 123; 2 Corinthians 1
4. Jeremiah 45-46; Psalm 124; 2 Corinthians 2-3
5. Jeremiah 47-48; Psalm 125; 2 Corinthians 4-5
6. Jeremiah 49-50; Psalm 126; 2 Corinthians 6-7
7. Jeremiah 51-52; Psalm 127; 2 Corinthians 8
8. Lamentations 1-2; Psalm 128; 2 Corinthians 9-10
9. Lamentations 3; Psalm 129; 2 Corinthians 11
10. Lamentations 4-5; Psalm 130; 2 Corinthians 12
11. Ezekiel 1-2; Psalm 131; 2 Corinthians 13
12. Ezekiel 3-4; Psalm 132; Galatians 1-2
13. Ezekiel 5-6; Psalm 133; Galatians 3-4
14. Ezekiel 7-8; Psalm 134; Galatians 5-6
15. Ezekiel 9-10; Psalm 135; Ephesians 1-2
16. Ezekiel 11-12; Psalm 136; Ephesians 3-4
17. Ezekiel 13-14; Psalm 137; Ephesians 5-6
18. Ezekiel 15-16; Psalm 138; Philippians 1-2
19. Ezekiel 17-18; Psalm 139; Philippians 3-4
20. Ezekiel 19-20; Psalm 140; Colossians 1-2
21. Ezekiel 21-22; Psalm 141; Colossians 3-4
22. Ezekiel 23-24; Psalm 142; 1 Thessalonians 1-2
23. Ezekiel 25-26; Psalm 143; 1 Thessalonians 3-4
24. Ezekiel 27-28; Psalm 144; 1 Thessalonians 5
25. Ezekiel 29-30; Psalm 145; 2 Thessalonians 1-3
26. Ezekiel 31-32; Psalm 146; 1 Timothy 1-2
27. Ezekiel 33-34; Psalm 147; 1 Timothy 3-4
28. Ezekiel 35-36; Psalm 148; 1 Timothy 5-6
29. Ezekiel 37-38; Psalm 149; 2 Timothy 1-2
30. Ezekiel 39-40; Psalm 150; 2 Timothy 3-4

in One Year

December

1. Ezekiel 41-42; Proverbs 1; Titus 1-3
2. Ezekiel 43-44; Proverbs 2; Philemon
3. Ezekiel 45-46; Proverbs 3; Hebrews 1-2
4. Ezekiel 47-48; Proverbs 4; Hebrews 3-4
5. Daniel 1-2; Proverbs 5; Hebrews 5-6
6. Daniel 3-4; Proverbs 6; Hebrews 7-8
7. Daniel 5-6; Proverbs 7; Hebrews 9-10
8. Daniel 7-8; Proverbs 8; Hebrews 11
9. Daniel 9-10; Proverbs 9; Hebrews 12
10. Daniel 11-12; Proverbs 10; Hebrews 13
11. Hosea 1-3; Proverbs 11; James 1-3
12. Hosea 4-6; Proverbs 12; James 4-5
13. Hosea 7-8; Proverbs 13; 1 Peter 1
14. Hosea 9-11; Proverbs 14; 1 Peter 2-3
15. Hosea 12-14; Proverbs 15; 1 Peter 4-5
16. Joel 1-3; Proverbs 16; 2 Peter 1-3
17. Amos 1-3; Proverbs 17; 1 John 1-2
18. Amos 4-6; Proverbs 18; 1 John 3-4
19. Amos 7-9; Proverbs 19; 1 John 5
20. Obadiah; Proverbs 20; 2 John
21. Jonah 1-4; Proverbs 21; 3 John
22. Micah 1-4; Proverbs 22; Jude
23. Micah 5-7; Proverbs 23; Revelation 1-2
24. Nahum 1-3; Proverbs 24; Revelation 3-5
25. Habakkuk 1-3; Proverbs 25; Revelation 6-7
26. Zephaniah 1-3; Proverbs 26; Revelation 8-10
27. Haggai 1-2; Proverbs 27; Revelation 11-12
28. Zechariah 1-4; Proverbs 28; Revelation 13-14
29. Zechariah 5-9; Proverbs 29; Revelation 15-17
30. Zechariah 10-14; Proverbs 30; Revelation 18-19
31. Malachi 1-4; Proverbs 31; Revelation 20-22

A Teen's Answers to Prayers

A prayer in its simplest definition is merely a wish turned Godward.

Phillips Brooks

Don't worry about anything; instead, pray about everything. Tell God what you need, and thank him for all he has done. If you do this, you will experience God's peace, which is far more wonderful than the human mind can understand. His peace will guard your hearts and minds as you live in Christ Jesus.

Philippians 4:6-7 NLT

Prayers and Answers

Prayers and Answers

Prayers and Answers

Prayers and Answers

Prayers and Answers

Prayers and Answers

References

All [personal promise] scripture verses have been adapted from the *King James Version* of the Bible (KJV). Unless otherwise indicated, all scripture quotations are taken from the King James Version of the Bible.

Scripture quotations marked AMP are taken from *The Amplified Bible, New Testament.* Copyright © 1958, 1987 by the Lockman Foundation, La Habra, California. Used by permission.

Verses marked TLB are taken from *The Living Bible,* copyright © 1971. Used by permission of Tyndale House Publishers, Inc., Wheaton, Illinois 60189. All rights reserved.

Scriptures marked NCV are quoted from *The Holy Bible, New Century Version,* copyright © 1987, 1988, 1991 by Word Publishing, Dallas, Texas 75039. Used by permission.

Scripture quotation marked NKJV are taken from *The New King James Version.* Copyright © 1979, 1980,1982, 1994, Thomas Nelson, Inc.

Scripture quotation marked PHILLIPS is taken from the *New Testament in Modern English,* (Rev. Ed.) by J.B. Phillips. Copyright © 1958, 1960, 1972 by J.B. Phillips. Reprinted by permission of Macmillan Publishing Co., New York, New York.

Scripture quotations marked NIV are taken from the *Holy Bible, New International Version*®. NIV®. Copyright © 1973, 1978, 1984 by International Bible Society. Used by permission of Zondervan Publishing House. All rights reserved.

Scripture quotations marked NRSV are from the *New Revised Standard Version of the Bible,* copyright © 1989 by The Division of Christian Education of the National Council of the Churches of Christ in the USA. Used by permission. All rights reserved.

Scripture quotations marked NLT are taken from the *Holy Bible, New Living Translation,* copyright © 1996. Used by permission of Tyndale House Publishers, Inc., Wheaton, Illinois 60189. All rights reserved.

Scripture quotations marked THE MESSAGE are taken from *The Message,* copyright © by Eugene H. Peterson, 1993, 1994, 1995, 1996. Used by permission of NavPress Publishing Group.

Additional copies of this book
are available from your local bookstore.

Also available:

My Personal Promise Bible for Graduates
My Personal Promise Bible for Women
My Personal Promise Bible for Mothers

If you have enjoyed this book,
or if it has impacted your life,
we would like to hear from you.

Please contact us at:

Honor Books
Department E
P.O. Box 55388
Tulsa, Oklahoma 74155
Or by e-mail at *info@honorbooks.com*